HOW TO SCAM

CORPORATIONS

by Lucas Anderssen

https://HowToScamCorporations.weebly.com

Copyright © Lucas Anderssen 2018. All rights reserved.

No part of this publication may be reproduced, stored in a retrieval system, or transmitted in any form or by any means without the prior written permission of the author.

This book is for informational and entertainment purposes only and is not intended to provide financial or legal advice. The author specifically disclaims any liability, loss or risk, personal or otherwise, that is incurred directly or indirectly as a result of the use of any of the information described in this book.

I learned the importance of using these words while working in Corporate America.

Second Edition

First Published in 2018

ISBN: 9781728891149

About the Author

I'm a middle-aged man living in Middle America. I will go out of my way to help people, even total strangers. Several times in my life I have found keys or phones or wallets loaded with cash and I've gone out of my way to get everything back to the rightful owner. I have done volunteer work for many years and have donated thousands of hours of my life and considerable amounts of money to them. I donate to charities regularly and tip generously. I have developed a life-long policy of never stealing from people, volunteer organizations or small businesses. I don't shoplift, I don't do carding and I don't steal identities. However, when it comes to dealing with corporations, I think everyone has the right to be opportunistic.

I have worked in multiple positions as an employee and as a manager in Corporate America for over twenty five years. Some years ago, I started to encounter techniques that employees were using to supplement their incomes and to get a tiny amount of revenge on corporations they worked for. I found out they looked at this as a part-time job that they were doing in addition to their day jobs. It turns out they have been able to use many techniques to profit from corporations, so I've been collecting these stories and decided to document them.

Table of Contents

Introduction 5
Part One: Being On The Inside 8
   Helping Others 8
   Helping Yourself 9
   Getting Into a Company 14
   Your First Day On the Job 16
   Embezzling Expenses 17
   Making Free Phone Calls 21
   Benefits Schemes 23
   Fake Your Own Death 24
   Kickbacks and Payoffs 26
   Be Reasonable 28
   Stealing Time 29
   Faking Disability 32
   Intellectual Property 35
   Suing Your Employer 36
   Planning for the Future 39
   Becoming a Whistleblower 42
   Leaving a Company 44
Part Two: Operating Outside A Company 46
   Techniques for Hijacking Corporations 46
      The Bustout 46
      The Shelf Corporation 47
      The Stock Scam 48
      The Ownership Change 48
      The Vanity Scam 49
      The Overpayment Scam 50
      The Building Hijack 50

The Fake Check	51
The Fake Corporation	53
Cyber Crime	55
Stealing from Restaurants	56
Insurance Scams	57
Getting A Debt Discount	59
Claiming Store Refunds	61
Class Action Lawsuits	63
Defrauding the Health Care System	68
Rebates, Promotions and Recalls	69
Getting Free Stuff by Complaining/Cajoling	72
Car Rental Companies	74
Conferences and Hotels	76
Social Engineering	79
Die!	81
Having A Lifelong Goal	83
Summary	84

INTRODUCTION

I'm a big believer in the capitalistic system that exists in the United States of America (USA). It's far from perfect, but it's better than many of the alternatives. What I do not approve of is the amount of power that now exists with companies and with their executives. We live in a time when the vast majority of power resides with corporations and with the wealthiest people in the USA. Individuals, unions, not-for-profit organizations and politicians may seem to have some level of authority in some cases, but for the most part it is an illusion. Corporate welfare, that is government subsidies given to prop up companies, benefit their executives and the richest in society. Employers now have a short term focus, driven by greed and desire for short term profits. Even though recent history has shown us that this approach has a devastating effect on the lives of many, there's one unavoidable fact: greed rules. Corporate takeovers and mergers are rife. Executives with minimal experience make outlandish promises to owners and investors in order to get funds, which ultimately line the executives' pockets and result in extreme pressures being placed on those below. When the promised profits don't materialize, scapegoats need to be found. Workers are laid off. Families suffer. Family members in need of health care benefits find they have no health insurance. Unable to take care of their family members, tension mounts, spouses divorce and lives degenerate into lifestyles of watching TV, eating alone and working 2 or more low paying jobs. People snap, resulting in behavior that ranges from antisocial to committing mass murder. The squeeze is on and it has been on for several years.

Corporations are evil. Wage theft, that is, theft of employees' wages by corporations, is at an all time high. Wage theft can take several forms, but mostly it consists of employers just not paying employees what they should be receiving. According to one study, the US dollar amounts of wage theft greatly exceed that of other crimes, like burglary and auto theft. Some store employees are required to keep working after they've clocked out. Immigrant workers are often not paid the full amount for the work they have done, as employers know they can get away with it. Temporary or seasonal workers also get abused in this way: they are promised a certain wage, then when they've done the work they get paid less. The sad fact is that there are many employers out there who simply do not treat employees with respect or dignity. Many companies are run by individuals who are out for their own gain, usually at the expense of the employee.

This book is unique. If you conduct a simple internet search looking for ways to scam corporations you won't get many hits. What you will see is page after page of information on how corporations are scamming us. Pick a subject that you are interested in and type that into an internet search box, immediately followed by "scam corporations" or "fraud" and you will see what I mean. In publishing this book I am trying to slowly turn the tables.

Corporations have paid my salary & helped me to maintain my lifestyle for a while now. But I have witnessed how badly employees have been treated at the hands of these beasts. I've seen good people tossed out onto the scrapheap of life at times when they needed employment or health care coverage the most, just because company profits were not where someone thought they should be. This is not a book about all the cruelty that I have seen happen in companies over the years, but I have written this to help you get. Get what? To help you to get what you want from corporations, especially those who you feel have wronged you in some way. Most of the getting described in these pages falls squarely under the heading of theft. You need to decide if this is what you want to do, based on your beliefs, principles and situation within a company. I have witnessed how successful some of the approaches have been for multiple people and I now want to share these techniques with you. I have included other schemes I have encountered as it seems like they would work if planned out effectively.

This is partly a How-To book. The other part is designed to get you to think. Creatively. I guarantee that using the insight I am giving you, you will come up with many more schemes. What you decide to do and how you do it will depend on the situations you find yourself in at any moment in time.

This book is written assuming that you live and work in the USA, but many of the principles hold true in other countries. The book is written in two parts: the first covers theft that can be carried out from working for a corporation. This is by far the easiest to accomplish as you have plenty of opportunities to see how things work from the inside and to take full advantage of those situations that you experience. The second part of the book addresses attacks you can make on companies from the outside. Let's go to work.

Part One: Being On The Inside

Helping Others

Here in the USA we live in an every-man-for-himself society. There is a safety net to help people who run into problems, financial or otherwise, but it has big holes in it. In other countries, mostly in Europe, the safety net is more intact to help people. Executives and senior managers are not so heavily rewarded as they are in the USA, relative to typical working people. You can argue the pros and cons of these different societies, but the reality is that we need to help each other much more in the USA, as governments are not so inclined to. As a result, I am advocating that when you are an employee for a company and you see someone embezzling, turn a blind eye. I have done this on numerous occasions. As a manager I wouldn't go out of my way to tell an employee to steal from the company, but if I saw something shady taking place I would deliberately let it happen, unless there was any risk of someone being hurt in some way. I had employees who needed some company product, so I let them take it. I've mentored fellow employees who wanted to start up their own business in direct conflict with our current employer. I've been aware of other coworkers who've taken items they needed and I don't rat out my fellow employee. I do this because it's the right thing to do. An added benefit is that they are less likely to rat me out.

What this means is that if you work in the finance department of a company and you suspect some employee fraud is happening, let it slide. Do you work in a hospital and see someone trying to cheat the system? Ignore it. Maybe you're a manager and you see an employee taking too much time off: let it happen. We all need to work together to help each other in subtle ways to beat the system. We can't allow total anarchy to take over. The companies we work for still need to function. However, helping each other out helps to level out the severely tilted playing field. If everyone was more like this I am convinced that the American society would be a better place.

Helping Yourself

Look around you. What do you see? What kind of security exists in the building where you work? In many cases you will find it easy to take home small items that are used around your work place on a daily basis. Slipping smaller items in pockets is more explainable if you are confronted than having items in a purse or bag. When walking out with items or taking anything that doesn't belong to you, be aware of how guilty you might look. Act confidently. Don't look shifty. Don't look around in a furtive way. Have an image in your mind that what you are taking is for legitimate purposes. Be prepared with a plausible explanation if confronted about what you are doing. Think about how you walk, act, talk & appear when you are not stealing company items and practice this when you're lifting from your employer too. As you walk out, visualize yourself doing what you enjoy the most, whether it's fishing, shopping or having sex. Your body language is critical to what others think of you. It's been said that when someone speaks they may or may not be telling the truth. But their body language does not lie.

If there's a first aid kit in your workplace, you shouldn't need to buy Band-Aids or antiseptic wipes at the store. Pens, tape and paperclips fit in your pockets easily. Notepads often look alike whether you bought them from a store or stole them from your employer. Does your cell phone need charging? Use your employer's electricity. Is free coffee available at work? Don't stop at Starbucks on your way in. Need batteries at home for electronics? You will probably find that your employer has some.

I don't advocate shoplifting, but a common trick used by established shoplifters is to wear baggy clothing to conceal items. Some creative shoplifters have fabricated some elaborate pants and skirts to cleverly hide large boxes. If you plan to use it, research this technique to make sure that what you wear doesn't give your game away. To be less conspicuous, wear baggy clothing regularly, even when you are not taking home items from your employer.

One of the best ways to avoid being caught is to take items that don't get counted or tracked in any way. Management doesn't care if you take a paperclip home from the office because nobody is counting them. Someone buys a big box, puts it in a cabinet and anyone can take what they need. When the box is empty somebody will buy another one. On the other hand, the company's finances are being tracked by a team of people and if money isn't where it should be, questions get asked. If it's a significant amount of money there will be an investigation. This is also true of expensive property owned by a company, referred to as capital assets. These are things with a large dollar value, such as photocopiers, company vehicles and production equipment. Capital items like these often have a tag or sticker on them with an asset code number. Think about the kinds of things you encounter that are not being tracked: towels and toiletries in hotel rooms; bowls, silverware, napkins and straws in restaurants; stationary items in an office; shop towels at a car repair shop. Once you have these at home it's unlikely anyone will come looking for them.

If you take something large that you know will be missed, think about the investigation that will take place. If you were the investigator what would you do? Who would you question and what approaches would you take? Suppose for a moment you embezzled some funds from the corporate coffers. What kind of paper trail did you leave behind you? Many paper trails are electronic in nature, so does this point to a computer that you use? Can you thwart this by using another computer? Are you taking money on your last day working for that company? If so how will they try to reach you? Did you lift a piece of equipment you plan to sell on eBay? Does it have a serial number? Did a security camera capture you? I have learned to put myself in the position of the other person over the years. This approach has served me well. Anticipate every question and every rabbit hole that investigators will go down. In many cases you only (!) have to survive six years, the statute of limitations in most US states for any kind of civil action to be taken against you.

I often need to photocopy documents at work for a volunteer organization I'm involved with. I have figured out the routines of my coworkers and boss and make sure I do this at a time and in a way that will avoid any confrontation from anyone. I stand at the copier with a folder containing work-related papers while I copy. As copies are spat out I carefully place them in my folder.

Don't discuss stealing company property with anyone. Trust nobody. You may think that someone there is your friend and that you can trust them, but you will sleep much better at night knowing that only you have the dirt on what you are doing. Many companies, especially those who have been crime victims before, will set up anonymous tip lines where people can rat out their fellow employees. Sometimes, to mitigate theft, managers will deliberately rotate employees from one role to another. This is partly to see if a theft problem disappears and partly as a matter of course to keep employees off balance and to keep them from being complacent. Other companies establish random audits, even if they have not seen theft issues. The point here is to be wary of managers and fellow employees at all times and not to divulge what you're up to.

Some employers try to minimize theft by instituting a code of ethics, which involves watching videos, regular training and re-training on topics relating to ethical behavior. They can tout this positively with customers and stockholders and it makes managers feel good and have something positive to talk about. This can be a good thing if you have your act together and know how to commit crimes. Managers feel more comfortable when they think you have gone through this training so might be less likely to suspect you of theft. Make sure you take the training and don't complain about it. Some companies want employees to take employee satisfaction surveys. These are carried out to gage how employees feel about all kinds of topics. Having been the survey taker on numerous occasions and been a manager reviewing the results I can say with confidence that these surveys are a total waste of time and money. Most managers feel obliged to deal with negative survey feedback and don't really care about having to make any changes to address problems that they reveal. I have never seen any changes come about as a result of employee opinion surveys. Most employees don't take them seriously, for good reason. However, if a high percentage of employees give very negative feedback on ethics issues this can raise a red flag that something needs to be investigated. You don't want this to happen. I usually fill out these surveys over a cup of coffee and do my best to give answers I think managers want to hear.

What happens if you are confronted about stealing? Be paranoid and expect it to happen at some point if you take items from your employer. Always be prepared to have a response for any situation so you don't appear flustered. Having some degree of plausible deniability is very important. If I was approached about my photocopying I'd openly admit that yes, I'm making these copies and thought the company was all in favor of helping volunteer organizations; I know other people do it. If I was asked why I was walking out with a box of papers at the end of the day I might smile and state that I'm going to a meeting the next day. If you have to travel to other company facilities you have a legitimate reason to take things out of the building, so use that to your advantage. Your exact situation will vary depending on the company, your position and other factors.

Some years ago a long-time employee was spotted pushing a wheelbarrow out of a facility. The security guard stopped him and asked him what was in the wheelbarrow. "Nothing", said the man. Not trusting him, the security guard closely inspected the wheelbarrow. Finding nothing suspicious he let the man go. Next day the same thing happened; yet again the guard could find nothing hidden in the wheelbarrow. When it happened for a third time, the security guard had the tire removed to see what was hidden inside: nothing. This went on for some time, then the man quit. Some time later the security guard spotted the man in a store and confronted him: "I know you were up to something; what were you stealing?" "Wheelbarrows" said the man.

Pilfering in plain sight can be done and this story illustrates that.

You might find that, despite all of your best efforts you get pulled into an unexpected meeting and confronted with some awkward facts or allegations about items you've stolen. Whenever you have to attend a meeting with your boss and human resources people, you should always be on your guard. Handle the meeting calmly and confidently without getting angry or upset. Don't cry or make any outbursts. Maintain your composure. If you are confronted with unavoidable facts, you don't want to insult the intelligence of others. But this is where you hope that your value to the company exceeds their desire to terminate you for theft. If you are fired, do your best to defend yourself. Ask yourself if you are able to take legal action against them, possibly due to discrimination or harassment. If so, bringing up this fact at the confrontation meeting might help minimize the risk of you being terminated for theft. This topic is covered in more detail later.

Where you are in the corporation affects what you can take. You might think that climbing the corporate ladder and becoming an executive will afford greater riches from scamming, but I have not seen this to be the case. Often it's the people towards the middle or below that have some level of authority they can abuse. The higher up you are in the corporate world, the more visible you are to subordinates. Most employees develop some kind of inner glow when they see the boss screw up as it reminds them that they too are human and fallible. So when employees see the boss embezzling, disgruntled employees tend to discuss it and report it. However, if you are an executive you will be responsible for large amounts of money and equipment, so your theft opportunities are greater in that respect.

Getting Into a Company

There is a legitimate way to gain employment: write your resume based on your education and experience, apply for vacant jobs that you see advertised, get dressed up and be interviewed. Then wait patiently. Or you can fake it. Create a fictitious name, fabricate a resume, schmooze your way through an interview and with a bit of luck get a job that you are not qualified for. Perhaps this approach worked in the 1960s, but in today's world of electronic checks of education and employment this is very difficult to pull off. And if you get the job, how will you be paid? Employers require a social security number and a legitimate bank account in your name. They need you to fill out a Department of Homeland Security Employment Eligibility Verification form (I-9) along with showing a valid ID within 3 business days of employees starting work.

What you might be able to do is to pad your resume. If you worked as a line supervisor, claim you were a manager. Lie about accomplishments and stretch employment dates. Use good friends to say great things about you, in exchange for favors or for you doing the same for them. I have acted as a reference for several friends looking to make career changes. Before their prospective employer calls me, I always find out what position they are applying for and some details about the job. This way I can talk creatively about how they'd be great at it and how they have been wonderful at doing similar functions in the past.

If you're going to lie on your resume (in some cases a criminal offense) you'll have more success doing it by fabricating information that's difficult to validate. Companies change ownership and change names all the time these days so claiming you worked for a small, obscure outfit, or an overseas operation, or one with several owner changes can often go uninvestigated. If you work on the assumption that whoever is doing pre-employment checks is lazy or overworked and looking for the path of least resistance you may be able to command a better starting position and salary in a corporation. Personally, when I'm pursuing a job change I don't like to answer questions about my salary. My goal is for them to want me. Then I will be in a much better position to command more money.

Be aware that when employers screen resumes they don't like to see long or multiple gaps in employment. Nor do they like to see a large number of short term gigs. A resume tells a story and you want that story to be a good one. If you have employment gaps, list consulting or volunteer work in those gaps. Sign up to be a volunteer for, say, the American Red Cross or the local food pantry. You don't have to actually do anything for them, but it can help to fill out resume gaps that might be hard to explain.

Remember that the goal of a resume is not to get you a job: it is to get you an interview. Once inside the door you need good interpersonal skills in the interview meetings. It's important to be liked and to appear energetic and enthusiastic. There are dozens of good books and resources that can help you with the more legitimate aspects of getting a job. But if you are going to be creative anywhere during the pre-employment process, be aware that if you get that job, you'll need to be able to do it to some extent or you won't last long. Then your ability to trick your way into a company won't matter.

Your First Day On the Job

You've applied for a job and secured it. You arrive for work early to meet with your new boss and with Human Resources. You want to become established and to create a good first impression. Your goal at this point is to be liked by your manager and his manager, without appearing to be a sycophant. Figure out what the job is, make sure you ask all the right questions and go out of your way to do the job well. Be aware that your manager has several influencers: people he respects in the organization whom he trusts to give him reliable information. Make sure that you are well respected by these influencers.

In any company, how you are perceived in the first couple of weeks is critical. Many companies will give you some kind of review about ninety days after you've started. In most cases, it is very easy for an employee to be laid off in the first ninety days of employment if things are not working out. When your manager is asked by her boss how you are performing, you want the answer to be positive. You want to come across as a clean, tidy, organized, professional person. Present an image of someone who is kind, considerate, courteous and conscientious. Things tend to become slightly easier for you as time goes on and this is when some self-centered creativity can begin.

EMBEZZLING EXPENSES

If you are fortunate enough to be able to buy items or to travel for your employer this is another great opportunity to line your pockets. Some companies will give you a credit card where they are billed directly for purchases you make. In some cases you will need to buy the items or pay for travel with your own credit/debit card, then file an expense report to get your money back. If you're given the choice it's often preferable to have someone else carry the debt, rather than yourself. However, sometimes there are more opportunities for expense embezzling if you pay for the items or the travel yourself, then submit an expense report to get reimbursed.

Make sure you understand the company's rules and policies before filing expense reports. Some companies have limits on hotel and travel costs depending on the city you stay in. All companies have budgets and are aware of how much was spent in the previous year on a specific set of items or by a department. Companies usually have a minimum expense amount, maybe $20 or $50, above which you need to submit a receipt to get reimbursed. They also have a deadline each month when expenses need to be submitted. Make sure you submit expenses every month, so that managers and the finance department get used to seeing your expenses. If the deadline to submit your expenses is, say, the last Friday of each month, make sure you submit them on that day. Your manager will be rushed to approve them by her deadline and is much less likely to scrutinize them. Your goal is to extract as much money as possible from the company without breaking them, without raising any red flags, staying within the rules and guidelines as much as possible.

Let's say you have to go on a business trip to a convention. You need to get to the airport, get on a plane, stay at a hotel, eat some meals, go to some meetings then come home after a couple of days. You could take a taxi to the airport; you could drive yourself, then pay to park there. Or you could just have a friend drop you off. Depending on the parking cost and the company's expense policy on receipts, the most lucrative deal for you might be to have a friend drop you off, but claim that you drove there and claim the parking expense. Understand how many miles it is from your house to the airport and increase this by about 10%, or by whatever you think will reasonably be accepted. Whenever you have to travel for business it should never cost you any money personally. Whenever you are paying for any meal or service that your employer will pay for, make sure you tip very generously.

If you have to pay for your own expenses and then get reimbursed, there are some creative tricks that can be used. For airfares, you could have the airline email you a copy of the receipt and use PDF-editing software to change the amounts. If an airfare is booked several weeks in advance it will be less expensive. Figure out what it would cost booked a few days before you travel and claim this amount. This can also be done with hotels: stay at a reasonably priced place, but claim for a larger amount by editing the receipt, within the company's guidelines, of course.

You will see me refer to PDF-editing software often in this book. It is one of the few tools you will need to buy to profit from the concepts I describe. PDF means "portable document format" and is an electronic format for saving documents which contain images and texts. There are many software types which can read a PDF & make it visible on your monitor or allow you to print it. However it takes special software to allow you to edit a PDF document. PDF-editing software is very powerful and useful for committing all kinds of fraud. If you want to edit a receipt or an invoice, you scan it, save it and then run an OCR (optical character recognition) utility that is built into the software. There are some free versions of these editing softwares, but I have not found any of them to be versatile enough. When I first started trying to manipulate documents I used some free software that converted the PDF to Microsoft Word, I edited in Word, then converted back to PDF. This was very cumbersome and usually gave major formatting issues where information was in the wrong place on the page or it just looked terrible for multiple reasons. Good PDF-editing software shouldn't give you these issues. OCR is especially powerful as it allows you to edit characters that might be recognized as pictures. You can convert these into text and in most cases have convincing looking documents. Expect to pay around $100 for some good software. Visit review websites to see which software is right for you.

I find meals are much easier to cheat with. Most companies will pay traveling employees for 3 meals per day, so make sure you claim for these. If they will pay, say, $30 without needing a receipt, submit each expense just under this without receipts. If someone else buys a meal for you, make a claim for that meal anyway, unless it's your manager. If your employer gives you a company credit card, make sure you use it, rather than paying cash for things.

If you need to rent a car while traveling, this is your chance to try a vehicle you would not normally drive. Again, understand what the limit is and stay within it; but only just. Also see the later section on car rental company scams. If you need to take a taxi, ask for a receipt. If you're paying with cash the taxi driver usually gives you a blank receipt. I prefer to fill these out as soon as I get out of the cab so I don't forget. Make sure you tip generously and write down a reasonably big number on the receipt. Embezzling taxi fares is easier than embezzling Uber rides: Uber payments are made electronically through credit cards, so are more traceable than cash payments made to taxis. However, if you are claiming expenses that you have paid yourself you can use PDF-editing software to change credit card statements.

Remember the importance of plausible deniability when embezzling; have responses planned out to issues that might come up. Here's an example of a scenario:

Salesman Joe is called into his manager's office after submitting his expense report.

Boss: "I see you made a charge on the company credit card at the Lonesome Cowboy Gentleman's Club. Can you explain this?"

Bad Response from Joe: "That wasn't me. I didn't make that charge."

Another bad response from Joe: "I lost my credit card so someone else must have done that."

Better response from Joe: "I had made arrangements to meet customer X there. I waited around but he didn't show up".

Even better response from Joe: "I met with the manager there and it looks like they are going to be a big new customer for our products. I'll have to go back there again next week to try to close the deal."

Some companies issue purchase cards (or P-cards) to employees who need to purchase large amounts of goods. Here again is another opportunity for some creative billing. Buy items for yourself, then figure out a way of reselling them. Need to order three new laptops for staff? Why not order four? Have items shipped to a vacationing coworker at another facility, but don't tell anyone. Intercept the item from the vacationer and resell it.

These are just a few approaches that can be taken when you have access to company funds. You will get creative and depending on your circumstances you will come up with many more.

Making Free Phone Calls

Companies often use conference call services so that their employees can connect with coworkers, suppliers and customers all over the world. They pay for a service, are given a phone number and purchase code numbers that come with leader personal identification numbers (PINs). Let's say a manager wants to set up weekly calls with his team members who are in numerous places around the world. He gives them the phone number and the conference code number to use to call in. The call can only start once the manager has entered his leader PIN, then everyone is connected. The company pays by the minute to the company that hosts the conference calls. Getting hold of this phone information is usually easy if you work in an office environment. Managers frequently pin this call information to their office wall. Sometimes they email it out to their employees so they can make calls without the manager's presence. Companies rarely check the usage history of these calls and managers are usually not even exposed to the billing process.

Once you have a manager's code number and PIN there are several things you can do with it. Share it with your friends so they can make free conference calls; this is especially useful for saving money on international calls, as domestic calls are almost free now, thanks to cell phones. You could sell the calling information to one of the company's competitors, who could call in when there are management calls happening. Senior management meetings are especially appealing in this case. Or you could have some fun and post the information online. Phone numbers that are used to call in to the service are obviously tracked so give this some thought before calling using your own personal phone.

Some years ago I obtained access to an executive secretary's online calendar. She had all of the executive's meetings on there and I gained access to his conference call information. I recall going out to a payphone and sitting in my car listening to one of their senior executive meetings. They discussed corporate strategy as well as completely inane topics. It was a real eye-opener.

Some companies offer cell phones to certain employees. They do this so they have the employee on a leash and can contact them. I like to refer to company-owned cell phones as tracking devices. The global positioning system (GPS) that's built into phones can be used to track your whereabouts. It's not a good idea to sneak out of work in the middle of the day and go to a bar with your phone on, just in case your manager decides to track your whereabouts. Turn it off in situations like this, leave it in the office or buy a faraday bag for it.

If your employer offers these phones, try to lobby your manager for one. The downside is that the company will often expect you to respond to calls and emails while you are on vacation. On the upside, you'll be able to make free personal calls, including international calls. You may be able to ditch your personal cell phone and just use the one your employer gives you. Alternatively you can carry two phones around with you wherever you go. You should be able to cancel your home internet service and use the company sponsored phone as a hotspot. When I was given a company cell phone I made sure to turn it off as soon as I left the office, unless I needed it for personal use.

BENEFITS SCHEMES

Many companies offer health insurance, dental care and other benefits to their employees, partly out of tradition, partly to keep their employees as healthy as necessary to do their work and partly because competitive companies are doing it. If you have a job that offers benefits, you are usually able to get insurance coverage for your spouse and children. When you are first hired you go through a process to register them and have them set up in your employer's database. This is where you need to ask yourself if there's anyone else you are close to who is in need of medical or dental coverage. Can you claim a girlfriend to be your domestic partner? Are you able to get a friend or cousin added to your benefits list as a dependant? Is there someone you can creatively add to your benefits package in exchange for, say, free accommodation, meals or cash?

When you register someone to be covered under your benefits package, it's usual for your employer to check some information of that person in a database. Make sure that you list accurate information about the person you are claiming as a dependent, as if they don't show up in the database you will have some explaining to do. If you can argue that your dependent was born overseas, so they don't have a SSN, this may be a loophole you can exploit. If you adopt or foster a child, the benefits company only needs the adoption documentation, so you should be able to claim a child as a dependent with fake adoption or foster papers. You shouldn't need to submit a SSN: someone only needs a SSN if they are applying to pay into the social security system.

Sometimes employers will carry out audits to make sure that those you are claiming as dependents really are eligible. If you have chosen to add dependents who are really not eligible, this is where you may need to creatively use PDF-editing software to fabricate the documents they are looking for. Deciding not to supply the requested information is a bad idea. Give them what they are asking for and make it look credible. The risk here is that if you are discovered providing fraudulent information, you could be asked to pay back any benefit money you have received. You could also potentially be terminated from your employment and be prosecuted for fraud. This requires careful planning and consideration, depending on your circumstances.

Fake Your Own Death

Insurance fraud has been taking place for as long as insurance companies have existed. The people at the insurance companies who investigate claims to make sure you are eligible are called Claims Adjusters and they are aware of every trick you could consider. When you make a claim it's in the company's interest to deny it as this will boost their profitability. One of the most complex insurance scams you can perpetrate is to fake your death so that your beneficiaries can claim on your life insurance policy. This is very difficult to do successfully in the USA, but slightly easier if you can arrange to fake your death and have a death certificate issued in another country. There are stories online of people who have obtained death kits from the Philippines, including death certificates. It could also be done in other developing countries. If you decide to go overseas to get a fake death certificate, research will be challenging and it's not something you can repeat if it goes badly. A better approach might be to have your partner-in-crime beneficiary submit a fake death certificate, fabricated with PDF-editing software. Doing this with official government documents is not easy due to the watermarks they often use, but can be done.

It's been said that faking your death by drowning is a bad idea. Insurance companies know that drowned bodies always wash up on a shore somewhere. Disappearing while hiking may be more readily accepted. It's also a good idea not to have your funeral staged as these can sometimes go awry.

Some employers offer life insurance policies at no charge, where beneficiaries would receive up to 100% of the employee's salary, or more by paying a small annual premium. The firms that administer this service for corporations are usually the same ones that administer other benefits. Just like any insurance company, they will have their own claims adjuster who will investigate the details of the death to make sure it's real. They will need a death certificate of the deceased person, which can usually only be given out once the identity of the dead body has been confirmed.

The authorities are more likely to issue a death certificate with no bodily evidence in situations where the person was exposed to "immediate peril". The State of New York issued death certificates for many people whose bodies could not be identified or found after the infamous September 11th 2001 attacks. This is also done for anyone thought to have been killed in battle. If there is no body or other proof of death, common law in most countries is to allow a death certificate to be issued seven years after the person is reported missing. If you claim on a life insurance policy and the person is later found alive you can expect to be sued, as well as to have to pay that money back.

One of the bigger challenges with faking your death is giving up everything you care about in your existing life. The older we get, the more attached we become to certain material items, even like certain items of clothing, jewelry and vehicles. It is also extremely difficult to give up on your loved ones, especially any children you may have, unless they are in on the fake death scheme. If they are conspirators, can you trust them? Another challenge is choosing the identity to use after your fake death. Once dead, your identity, SSN, credit and passport are essentially wiped clean. Do you have another ID that you can live under, possibly one you have legitimately borrowed from your friend or family member who has agreed to share it with you?

Kickbacks and Payoffs

Depending on your role in the company, you may be eligible to receive payoffs from suppliers or customers. Let's say you are a manager of a shipping department at a manufacturing company. Freight companies will offer to take you to lunch and bring you gifts in the hope that you will keep sending business their way. This is normal and is how business is done in most western societies. Some of these gifts can be trivial, like pens or doughnuts, but if you forge a good relationship with a supplier, you can make them an offer. Make it clear that you, and only you, are responsible for deciding which freight companies are used. Explain that right now you use 4 freight companies, but if the supplier is willing to pay you personally, off the books, that you will drop one of the other firms and send that business to them. Explain also that your employer treats you OK, but doesn't pay you what you need to support your lifestyle with five children, a sick wife and a dying mother. Make it clear that you are an otherwise decent person, looking for ways to bring in additional income. Gain the sympathy of the supplier. I have seen this approach work, but it comes with the obvious challenges. What happens when you go on vacation and someone else has to do the job and asks questions about your modus operandi? How long can you keep up this deceit? Do you find operating these schemes to be a thrilling challenge or do they keep you up at night? Anything that pulls so heavily on your conscience that makes you sick is probably not worth pursuing. But approaching something like this with the enthusiasm of an entrepreneur can give you a huge rush and be rewarding both financially and emotionally.

    The healthcare system is especially rife with stories of kickbacks due to the huge amounts of money at stake in that industry. Doctors have been known to take payments from drug manufacturers to promote their products. In some cases doctors have made millions of dollars by prescribing questionable medications so they could be paid off by the drug companies. Some of these kickbacks have been monetary, disguised as speaking fees or payments for attending advisory meetings; some have been expensive trips, televisions and other consumer goods. In some cases doctors have accepted monies for referring clients to specific hospitals, clinics and other health care facilities. When your doctor prescribes a medication or refers you somewhere, you need to make sure you are a well-informed patient and look out for your own best interests. Do not think that just because your doctor is politely spoken, clean-cut and well educated that he is above taking payoffs from deep-pocketed corporations.

BE REASONABLE

When taking from employers, do your best to be reasonable about it. Don't destroy the company in doing so. Don't be wasteful, taking things that you'll just throw out.

Not too many years ago, the vice president of finance at Koss Corporation, an electronics company, creatively embezzled $34 million over a period of several years and is still in federal prison as of this writing. She used the money to pay for her lavish lifestyle of clothes and vehicles. As a result employees suffered, pay was cut and some employees were laid off. The full story can be read online. I am not condoning this level of fraud which can destroy a corporation or hurt employees. I believe in a lower level of activity, taking a much smaller percentage of the company's wealth. In the case of the Koss fraud, the $34 million was about one year's turnover for the company and represented nearly half of its pretax profits over the fraud period. One of the ways she was able to get away with her acts for so long was that even though she needed to have her boss's approval to pay invoices over $5,000, no approval was needed to issue cashier's checks or wire transfers: the main way in which the funds were taken. Understanding how she was able to exploit this loophole may give you other ideas as you look at your own personal situation in a company. She became totally consumed with the embezzling that she couldn't stop. When she was finally caught she was completely relieved. Make sure that whatever theft you conduct is under your control and that you can stop at any time.

STEALING TIME

Your time is the most valuable thing you have. Once it's lost it will never return. There are a lot of conscientious folk out there who work excessive hours and want everyone to see that they work hard. That is not your objective. Your goal is to get the job done but most importantly it is to take care of yourself first. If you are an hourly-paid (non-exempt) employee, you could have someone else clock-in or out for you every now and again. You could help them out in the same way. When the cat's away the mice will play, so take full advantage of your freedom when your boss is out of the office. Can you leave early for an appointment without disrupting the work of others too much? Can you develop a health problem that requires regular doctor visits? Get creative based on the situation you find yourself in.

Employers usually allow employees to take time off for occasional sickness. Make sure you use up all sick days you are given. When calling in sick it's best to call within a few minutes of waking up; this is when your voice will be most raspy and you will sound at your worst. Even though most companies don't have a definition of sick for the purpose of taking these days off, you don't want your boss to think you are just taking a day off to go to the amusement park with your friends. When I call in I never describe the problem. I will tell my manager that I need to take a sick day, or state that I'm feeling under the weather so sorry, I can't some in. If my boss asks about my problem I give a generalized response, indicating I would prefer not to discuss the personal nature of my health. A number of companies do not allow non-exempt employees to take sick days immediately after a public holiday or after already scheduled paid time off, so be careful how you handle this situation.

I was once an unhappy employee looking to find another job somewhere else. I'd been there a few years and had a good reputation for doing quality work. Once I started my job search I started explaining to my manager that I was having some major personal issues at home and that I wouldn't be able to travel overnight in the foreseeable future. Once I had identified a position that looked promising I stressed to him again that I was having some deeply personal issues and that I might need to take some time off in the future. I'm known by everyone as someone who keeps himself to himself, so he didn't pry or ask what my issues were. If he had asked me, I would have politely told him that I couldn't discuss the details. After a while I was offered the new job, so I told my existing boss that my personal problems had escalated and would it be OK if I worked from home for a while? I explained how things would work out & what I would do. He was sympathetic and immediately agreed. I started my new job while I was still on the payroll at my former company. This worked out well for a number of reasons. My new employer didn't offer medical benefits until I'd been there for 30 days. My old company was due to pay me a decent bonus that I wanted to get. If you know anything about bonuses you know that you have to be on the payroll on the day the payments are made or you don't get them. I also wanted to have as much income as possible. After a couple of weeks I started to get phone calls from my old boss, asking for me to call him. I had told my family that if anyone called asking for me they were to say: "He's not here right now; can I take a message?" I ignored all the calls. Eventually my boss's boss started to call me. Then one day the bonus checks were cut and I was eligible for benefits at the place I had been working at for over a month. So I called my former manager and handed in 2 weeks notice. They were exciting times.

This kind of co-employment can be conducted many ways. A friend's husband was at a job he didn't like so he took a leave of absence and went to work somewhere else, where he was paid a big signing bonus. He worked there for a while, but realized he actually preferred his previous job. So he went back to it and kept the signing bonus. I have seen employees accept a job with another company for more money, then wave that offer in their manager's face, demand they match the higher salary and get it. A manager will only fall for this approach once with any given employee.

If you have a job where you don't need to physically be at an office all the time, say in sales or delivery, this is often a perfect opportunity to set up and run a business on the side, work a second (or third) job or to take other liberties, depending on your desires. This is something I have done several times and it can be very rewarding. There are many books on the subject of running a part-time business, but what's important is to do something you are passionate about. Let's say you trade antiques on eBay: is this something you can do at work, creating the illusion you are doing what your manager thinks he is paying you for? If you are in sales, can you work two sales jobs at once?

You run the risk of losing credibility if both sales jobs are in the same industry, calling on the same clients, but if managed well you could take two completely different sales jobs where each management expects you are working forty hours per week, but you work each job four to five hours per day and come out ahead.

One of the reasons that most employees feel like trapped slaves is that they think like consumers. They assume that working for The Man is all they are capable of. Breaking out of that thinking is critical to breaking away from corporate slavery. Think like a producer, someone who is making and selling things into society, rather than as just a consumer or a doer of other people's tasks. Think of the kind of corporate theft I have described in these pages as a first step towards that freedom.

FAKING DISABILITY

Make sure that you fully understand your employer's policy on short-term and long-term disability as this is something else that can be gamed. If you become temporarily disabled and unable to work, say in a car accident or due to some surgery or illness, many companies will pay you while you go through your recovery. They will usually expect you to use up any unused vacation time for that year first as paid time off. If you still need time off after this they will allow you to take a certain number of weeks off as short-term disability (STD). Usually, STD will pay you up to 60% of your base pay for up to 4 months. If you need time off after this, you may then be able to take time off under their long-term disability (LTD) policy, usually at a lower salary percentage than with short-term disability. LTD payments are usually up to 50% of your base salary, but you can sometimes buy some additional insurance to extend that slightly when you sign up for company benefits each year. Many companies often don't have the resources to administer disability, so will outsource it to another company, who will offer this service to multiple other firms. This third-party company will have their own expectations of you that they have negotiated with your employer, so make sure you know what these rules are too.

Companies realize that employees will sometimes fake or exaggerate their medical conditions, which is why they pay you less of your salary while you are on disability. They know you want to be making your full salary, not a percentage of it, so they have established this system. But supposing you are legitimately sick or need time off to take care of some things and are willing to work for less pay? Maybe you want to explore another employment opportunity. Maybe your side business is ramping up. Or maybe you want time off to write a book. Taking short-term disability can often be a convenient way to accomplish this, as long as you are fine with the reduced income.

Taking advantage of a company's disability allowances usually requires some social engineering to be carried out. First, if you know you have surgery coming up, I find it's best to tell people you work with. This allows for some sympathy to kick in: both managers and fellow employees will start expecting less output from you. This will also allow the boss to start reallocating work if needed, which will ease the stress on those who will have to pick up your slack when you are gone. Making people aware of your condition, assuming you have one, will make it easier to take extended time off if you choose to, as everyone will already know you're not doing so well anyway.

Lying to the boss and especially to your coworkers can be the most difficult part. When most of us hear that a coworker is not doing well we want to express concern and see if we can help. To minimize any guilt, you are better off exaggerating a condition, rather than totally fabricating something. Most people, when they hear of a sick colleague, encourage them to take all the time off work that they need. Take full advantage of these sympathies by doing exactly that.

If you choose to totally fabricate disability to get time off, it will be easier if this is done suddenly and without any warning. If you decide you were in a fictitious car accident, make sure it's far away from home, making it difficult for coworkers to visit you. If you can arrange for your sudden accident or illness to happen in another country, that would be even better. Have surgery & recuperate in another state. Many people know that some hospitals such as Mayo Clinic or those in Houston provide top-notch care, so it should be no surprise to them to learn that you are many miles from home getting good care at one of these facilities. You may not actually be at these places, but creating the illusion that you are can work in your favor.

In order to substantiate your short or long-term disability, the company that your employer has engaged to manage this function for them will require some documentation. You will need to provide doctor's notes and sometimes dates of surgeries. Make sure you know what condition you are exaggerating, understand all its symptoms and, if necessary, take medications to exaggerate these. Alternatively, if you are taking medications, you may be able to come off them for a while to fake symptoms. When you visit the doctor to initiate a disability claim, make sure that you look at your worst. Don't bathe, wear old, ripped clothes, walk slowly and deliberately or get yourself a wheelchair. If you are male, don't shave. Don't take illegal drugs as these can be found in drug tests, but otherwise do whatever it takes to get your doctor to believe your story.

In some cases the doctor's office may be contacted directly for verification, so do your research and make sure that you cover all the angles. If the doctor's office doesn't need to be contacted, but you have to provide documentation yourself for a fake or exaggerated illness, you may need to adjust some documents using your friend the PDF-editing software, depending on what is being asked for and what you can offer. Usually while you are on STD your medical and other benefits continue as normal. Once you go onto LTD, however, these usually only last for a few months or so, after which you will need to pay the COBRA rate. COBRA, or Consolidated Omnibus Budget Reconciliation Act of 1985, is a law that mandates that employees can get health insurance coverage after they leave their employers. Unfortunately, the cost of this is the full amount of what the employer pays, which will be several times what you, the employee, pays.

Some companies have restrictions and exclusions that apply when making disability claims. For example, if your illness was pre-existing before joining the company, or if you had a self-inflicted injury, you may not get coverage. Make sure you read all the fine print before going down the road to claim disability money. In some cases you may be better off claiming social security benefits for a long term illness or disability. You can game this in a similar way, but the government will have different requirements and it can take a long time to get a claim verified. If your performance is suffering at work and you think you might be disciplined or possibly terminated, make sure you tell your employer about health or disability problems immediately. It is more difficult to be terminated if you have a documented disability than if you are just seen to be incompetent or lazy.

Intellectual Property

One of the most valuable things a company has is not necessarily its facilities or equipment, but its intellectual property, or IP. This includes things like customer lists, expertise on making the company's products, patents, lists of employees and their capabilities, as well as knowledge of how the company provides services to customers.

If you are exposed to a company's IP it is worth collecting it, wherever possible. If you stay in that employer's industry it can be very valuable in the future, even if it is not up to date. Let's suppose you are in the finance department and encounter sales, customer and profitability information. That would be useful for you to have if you went to work for a customer, supplier or competitor. Many companies don't want to overtly buy stolen IP and this is not something that you can openly advertise as your reputation could be severely tarnished. However, if handled creatively, this information can be sold by setting yourself up as a consultant, ideally with an alternate name.

Creating an alternate name for business purposes is easy. If your name is John Blub you can open up a Doing-Business-As (DBA) business account at a bank in the name of, say, Eric Curtains. To open up the account you'll need to provide your real SSN, date of birth and address, but as far as the client is concerned you are Eric Curtains. This reminds me of my favorite joke. A man placed an announcement in a newspaper: Mr. Norman Penis wants to inform everyone that he is changing his name; effective immediately, he will be known to everyone as Norm Penis. I digress.

IP can also be invaluable if you set up a company to compete with your employer. If you think this might be something you'd like to do, it's best to start slowly taking information a piece at a time as you come across it and cataloging it in a secure place. Trying to gather all the information you need in a day or so can prove to be very difficult and risky. Keep track of what you need and what you have actually taken. Stealing IP can be no more difficult than stealing office supplies if done correctly. In many cases it can be transferred onto a portable USB drive. When you get home, transfer it onto a computer. Companies keep logs of every electronic event that takes place, including the movement of information to portable drives. Unless you are working for the government they rarely do anything about it.

Suing Your Employer

There are numerous ways for an employer to get rid of an employee and in some cases you can take legal action against them to claim damages if you feel you have been unfairly dismissed. Sometimes there's a downturn in the company's fortunes and they look at their financial statements and decide to shave a certain dollar amount or dollar percentage off the expense line. Sometimes a manager just doesn't like an employee so he decides she has to go. On occasions an employee is let go after being discriminated against: maybe the boss thinks that the employee is too old to handle things or that a black woman can't do the job. If you are suddenly summoned into an unexpected meeting with your manager and a human resources (HR) representative you need to cautiously assume the worst: that you are about to be terminated. In some cases your boss's manager will also be involved and sometimes it will be just HR. I have come across situations where employees have been let go en masse: called into a room and all told to be out by a certain time. I have heard of a case where a large team was called into a meeting and told that some of them would be let go. They were to go back to their workstations and wait for a possible phone call. If they were to stay with the company they would not be called. There have been many situations where a large group is offered early retirement: they get to go home early and be paid a pension or a severance package in exchange for signing a document and not coming back.

The first thing to realize with any of these situations is that they are usually negotiable. So many times employees are offered a severance package and think it sounds great, so they sign the document that is put in front of them. It's in writing on company letterhead, so it must be official, right? Do not sign anything until you have had time to think about it. In the case of redundancies in force (RIFs) where the company feels they need to let go of a large number of the work force or they will go under, they will just pull you into an office individually, explain the situation, ask you to sign the document and lead you to believe that this is a good deal. They want you to accept it and will tell you that others have also been asked to leave under similar circumstances. Your best bet in this situation is to be seen as a minority: being a young white male does not put you in a strong situation if you want to start any legal action against the company.

After being presented with the severance package and the document to sign, your best bet is to make sure you fully understand what you have been told, pick up the document, say nothing and walk out. This will give you time to think about the specifics of your situation. You have to decide if you want to stay employed there – possibly not – or if you would like to take legal action. In order to take legal action your first step is to contact the Equal Employment Opportunity Commission (EEOC), visit their website, eeoc.gov or to contact an employment attorney. The EEOC is a federal agency that administers and enforces workplace discrimination. You can take legal action against your employer if you feel you have any argument whatsoever that you have been discriminated against based on race, skin color, religion, sex (including pregnancy, gender identity and sexual orientation), national origin, age, disability or genetic information. Be aware that employment regulations vary from state to state. If you decide to fabricate or exaggerate some discrimination to strengthen your case, be aware that the person you are claiming discriminated against you will undergo questioning and possibly disciplinary action, maybe including termination. You can also sue your employee if you are terminated for refusing to perform an illegal act, or if your employer makes your work environment so uncomfortable that you feel forced to quit.

The EEOC website is excellent and has all kinds of useful information that you should be aware of before you get called into that unexpected meeting. It's required reading for anyone working for an American company. There is an especially good section on Prohibited Employment Policies/Practices which describes how employers are not allowed to discriminate, including during the job advertising, recruitment, employment or termination processes. We've all heard about sexual harassment, but harassment for any reason relating to the above factors can give you a strong legal case to sue. Sometimes the act of starting legal action either through the EEOC or with an attorney can result in you and the company reaching a settlement, with you being better off.

If you decide to take legal action, make sure you have all your facts documented. It helps if you file a grievance with the company, so make sure you know what the process is to do this. Keep written records relating to dates when discrimination occurred, who was involved and what was said and done. If there were emails, make sure you get copies of these as soon as incidents occur. Once you have left the company it will be close to impossible to go back and get information to strengthen your case. Keep all copies of pay stubs, performance appraisals and any other accolades you may have that highlight what a great employee you were. Make sure you have these at home, not in a filing cabinet at work. Try to get fellow employees to act as witnesses to what you are making a claim about, preferably in writing. Document discussions with management and HR in writing and follow up with emails stating a summary of discussions. If you are asked to provide any documentation to the company you are suing, make sure you give them copies and keep the originals in a safe place.

Be aware that trying to sue your employee is not an easy thing to do. Don't bother taking legal action against them just because you've been treated unkindly. The employer must have broken the law in some way and you must have been harmed for the legal case to have any merit. Be aware too that companies get sued regularly, so are used to handling cases. It might be your first time, so you will not be as experienced as them at the legal process. Legal action is usually a long, drawn out, slow process, often taking years to complete. Make sure you have the patience and stomach for it before moving forward. Be sure you don't have any skeletons in your closet, or if you do that they are well hidden. How many times have you been fired before? Were you caught embezzling from your previous employer? These kinds of things could well come out in the wash. If you are claiming for any kind of emotional distress along with the way you were discriminated against, expect some other aspects of your personal life to be exposed. But if you are convinced you have a case against them, find a lawyer who has handled cases against corporations before, dig in and fight them.

Planning for the Future

While you are working at a company, don't restrict your thinking to what is available today. Be aware of what you might be able to extract from them in the future. Do they give extra benefits to employees who stay for, say, five years? Are stock options, pension rights or annuities available? How might you take advantage of a company even after you've departed for one reason or another?

Some years ago a friend of mine worked for a large corporation and when he quit he did what everyone should do: he made sure he got every penny he was entitled to, as well as a few extra. Some years after he'd left, he had an unexpected letter from them, telling him he was entitled to pension benefits. When he looked through the package it was obvious they had him confused with another person with the same first and last names. This was a big company so he saw how this could happen, as his name is somewhat common. The papers gave him a set of instructions as to which options to chose: lump sum or different annuity options and how to sign the forms, get them notarized and send them back to the pension benefits administrator. Now, he knew he was not entitled to the benefits they described, but what did he have to lose? He followed the instructions and mailed the documents back. A couple of weeks later the pension benefits administrator mailed him back all his papers with a cover letter regrettably informing him that they had him confused with someone else. So sorry, but he wasn't entitled to anything that he hadn't already received.

At this point many people would have given up and thrown the papers in the trash. Instead he called the company and asked to speak to the pension benefits manager (the administrator's boss). He politely explained that he had some pension papers to submit and could he please send them to her to process? No problem, she told him. He obtained her name and location within the company. He typed out a very nice formal cover letter addressed specifically to her, requesting that she please process the enclosed forms. He mailed everything to her specifically and not too long after this he received a nice check in the mail, which he promptly deposited into an IRA account. He still has the money: even though this company knows which bank the money went to, they legally can't withdraw it from his account without his approval.

Why did this work? Why was he able to get this money from them that he was not entitled to? He was betting on a number of things falling into place. First, he was betting that the pension benefits administrator didn't tell her boss when she first mailed him someone else's paperwork. When you make a mistake at work do you tell your manager? You probably don't. If you're like most people, when you realize you've messed up you clean up the mess you made and keep quiet about it. If you tell your boss every time you make a mistake it won't be too long before they let you go. You cover things up to protect yourself. This aspect of employment is something that can be taken advantage of in many ways. Catch an employee at a corporation making a mistake in your favor and there's a decent chance you'll get away with it. Employees care more about their own skins than about company assets. I know that I do.

Second, he was betting that the pension benefits manager was not good at delegating. I have seen this with some managers, who are so autocratic and pompous, that they feel they have to do everything themselves. If she were a good manager, she would have handed his paperwork to the administrator when she received it and it would have been denied right there. The administrator is supposed to handle and process the forms and submit them to her boss for approval. The manager then submits the payments for processing. His application skipped a layer of approvals.

Third, he was betting that the other ex-employee with the same name as him didn't submit his paperwork before my friend's was processed. Now, my friend knows this company and is sure that when the other guy submits his paperwork, they will pay him. Legally they have to. I can just imagine the lively discussion in the office when his paperwork arrives with the administrator and is submitted for approval.

Several months later, when the manager realized that my friend had money he wasn't entitled to, she wrote him a stern letter, explaining the misunderstanding and demanding he pay them back with interest. That letter went straight through my friend's shredder. At this point he made the same assumption that he had made before: that she wouldn't be telling her manager about the missing money. It's one thing to send the wrong papers to someone, but to send money to the wrong person is very much frowned upon in companies. It seems he was right: a number of years later he hasn't heard from that company any more and has the statute of limitations working in his favor. It's just as well he has no plans to work there ever again. Many companies don't offer pensions these days, but if you work for such a place you might be able to figure out how to intercept pension payout information from them in other ways.

    Planning for the future can also include getting information on the potential benefits that others may be entitled to. You don't want to deprive a fellow worker of any of these benefits, but if you can fraudulently make claims on their benefits, the employer will still be required to pay them, while you may have been able to intercept money and run off with the company's funds.

Becoming a Whistleblower

The government (state and federal) is also very keen to take advantage of corporations in some situations. In fact, they will grant protection to individuals who blow the whistle on corporate wrongdoing where the government is losing out, such as in cases of Securities and Exchanges (SEC) fraud or taxation issues. If you find your employer is breaking the law and, especially if you feel they are in some way taking advantage of the government, you can report this to an attorney and if the case is successful you can get up to 30% of the proceeds. In the last five years the US government has paid out over $107 million as rewards. A relatively recent payout was to a Monsanto executive who benefited to the tune of around $22 million after he blew the whistle on the company which was found guilty of SEC fraud and forced to pay over $80 million.

In another recent case, Genesis Healthcare Inc. was required to pay almost $54 million to reconcile claims that they provided medically unnecessary care and that the care they provided was substandard. In addition they allegedly billed the government for this. Seven whistleblowers received almost $10 million as a result of the company's violations of the False Claims Act. The company suffered and the whistleblowers gained.

There are several federal laws which provide protection to the blower and stipulate that rewards are paid. These include the False Claims Act, the Dodd-Frank Financial Reform Act, the Occupation Safety and Health Act (OSHA). Some states have their own laws that offer protection and rewards to employees who report fraud at the state level. The Internal Revenue, SEC and Commodity Futures Trading Commission (CFTC) also offer protection and rewards.

Just like suing your employer, blowing the whistle on corporate malfeasance is not easy. You need to hire an attorney, be prepared to be discovered (even though you will have protection from termination or demotions or other punishment). Just identifying the problem usually isn't enough. Whistleblowers usually have to work hard to provide significant evidence to the government and expend a lot of energy to keep the case going, all the while not being sure they will actually win out and gain financially at the end of the day. If you see wrongdoing at a corporation you need to decide if you want to tell an executive or blow the whistle through an attorney. This is not a do-it-yourself process and certainly needs professional legal help to navigate the minefield. There are law firms who specialize in cases like this and would be the best ones to start with, rather than approaching a generalist lawyer.

LEAVING A COMPANY

Everyone ends up leaving a company for one reason or another, whether it's voluntarily or involuntarily, for another job, to set up a company or to retire. If you leave voluntarily you will want to take as much of the company's property with you as you can, whether it's intellectual property, funds or just office supplies. The best time to gather up what you plan to take is before you announce your departure to anyone.

If you're planning to leave your employer I find it's best to avoid even hinting that you might be leaving. I like to openly tell my boss that I love working there and that I plan to be there forever. I once had a manager who told me I could totally trust her and that if I was ever planning to leave the company I should just go to her and discuss it. I wonder how many people fall for that. Once you tell your manager you're looking into leaving they immediately start planning to replace you in one form or another. Word spreads like wildfire throughout the organization that you're leaving. One person tells another in confidence, who then tells another, in confidence. It's not long before people you've never met come up to you in the corridor and tell you they are sorry to hear you're leaving, even when you haven't even secured another job. If you genuinely feel that you can negotiate a better deal by threatening to leave, think long and hard about that strategy. Your instincts will tell you the extent to which you can negotiate. Only announce to your manager that you are leaving once you know you have secured your future and that, if you are going to another job, that you have passed any pre-employment screening.

Once you quit, you can expect the unexpected. Employees often feel like they should do the decent thing and give two or more weeks' notice. If you have a unique skill, employers may ask you to work out your notice or try to get you to stay for longer while they find your replacement. For specialized positions it's often very difficult to find a replacement in two weeks. Sometimes employers will decide that you are leaving within minutes of you giving notice and that they will only pay you until the end of that day. You should assume this could happen, even though you feel like you're doing the right thing by giving a couple of weeks' notice.

It's always worth being aware of how other employees are treated when they quit. If they are treated badly, there's a good chance you will be too. For professional positions it's common to be escorted to your office to gather up your personal items when you quit, then escorted off the property. The manager then instructs human resources to pay you until the end of the pay period. This has happened to me twice. What this means is that you should be very aware of the pay cycles within a company and make sure you can maximize your income around them. Don't hand in your notice the day before a pay cycle ends unless you have a good reason.

Managers often feel like they need to give the impression they are in charge and in control. If other employees see the boss escorting you out of the building they assume that the boss has initiated the termination. That just reinforces the image that they are in charge. Managers usually don't want to give the impression that a subordinate is calling the employment shots. Once you've left, managers often tell your former coworkers that you are "no longer with the company" or that you "left to pursue other interests". They feel that this politically correct jargon gives the impression you were terminated by the boss, whether it's true or not.

Whichever way you look at your situation, if you are planning to leave, you need to take anything and everything that will be useful to you at least a day before you make the announcement. This includes any of your personal items, as it will probably be difficult to go back to get anything you forget.

Part Two: Operating Outside A Company

Frequently the best way to target a company for funds is to be on the inside. It's easier to see how the place operates and the specific targets you can hit. However, there are a number of ways to extract money from outside the corporation as a non-employee. Here are a few of these, but remember my philosophy of not targeting small businesses: only go after larger corporations that can absorb the hit.

Techniques for Hijacking Corporations

I've listed out here approaches that have been taken over the years to target and possibly hijack companies for short term gain.

The Bustout

In a bustout, you obtain large amounts of merchandise from a company without paying for it. This is accomplished by setting up a small company and buying small amounts of merchandise and paying promptly to establish good credit. Then you make larger and larger purchases, still paying on time until one day you make the largest purchase ever, but fail to pay. You sell the inventory online or to other businesses, possibly through another business you have established. This type of fraud requires a lot of planning and can require considerable funding.

If you are going to steal items from a company for resale, studies have shown that the best types of products to focus on are small items, as they are easier to move. It's best of they are general consumer items such as housewares, TVs, stereos, computers, apparel and health & beauty aids. If you steal unique, specialized pieces of equipment you may have trouble selling them and be stuck holding onto them for a long time.

Let's say for example you want to target a company that produces small consumer electronics products. You could set yourself up as a small, local distributor and get credit established with the manufacturer. Start by buying a few items, selling them for a small profit, close to your cost. Each month place an order larger than the previous month, making sure you are actually moving your inventory and not being saddled with it. Understand the payment terms to your supplier and make sure you pay on time or early. Once you reach a point where you have established yourself as a good business person with a good track record, place a huge order and wait for it to arrive. That's when you disappear with the inventory and sell it through a different channel under an alternative name. You can take this approach with multiple suppliers at the same time to maximize the benefit.

One of the problems with consumer electronics products is that sometimes they have traceable serial numbers. Before pursuing this approach you'll want to make sure this will not cause you any problems. Some larger TVs and other more expensive electronic items contain tracking devices. Be of aware what you are taking and how it can track your movements.

The Shelf Corporation

A shelf corporation is a shell or paper company that is legally formed, then put on the shelf until it's needed for other purposes. The people setting them up are required to demonstrate some activity, so they open a bank account and may do some minimal trading and file tax returns. They do have legitimate purposes, but you can set one up and use it for criminal gain. If there was a company you wanted to target, you could create or buy a shelf company with a similar name to the one you are targeting. Then you could use it to impersonate that company and deceive suppliers and customers to get inventory, which you can resell or take their receivables (money owed by other companies).

Another approach with a shelf company is to slowly build up the paper company to look like a well-established, credit-worthy business by essentially self-reporting fake credit reports. You can then use this to establish large lines of credit with other companies. Once you have the funds or inventory you need from these companies you disappear, leaving a trail of defrauded businesses, lenders and creditors. They try to go after the shelf company, only to find an emptiness with no money and no assets.

To add credibility to scams like this it's important to have a professional, impressive looking website. It helps to have confidence marks on your site. These are symbols or logos, indicating the company has been vetted and verified by the more prestigious organization, which you would steal from more legitimate sites. Verified by Visa would be an example. You also need a system of telephone numbers, such as using disposable cell phones, or "burners". It's also worth setting up a Voice over Internet Protocol (VoIP) telephone service, where you can obtain any number in any location. All these phone systems can be programmed to have the name of your shelf company appear as the caller-ID name.

Another way to improve your credibility is to have a virtual office with an actual person who answers the phone for you, greeting the caller with the name of your shelf company. These can come with a prestigious sounding address, such as on Wall Street, New York. Mail, including checks and packages, can be sent there and forwarded on to you or you can have them collected.

The Stock Scam

With this approach, you establish a fictitious company, then exchange its worthless stock for the stock of a sound company. You create false financial statements with inflated assets. These statements are used to get other businesses to exchange stock for a piece of a bogus holding company. The assets of a legitimate company acquired in this way are then sold off or used as collateral on bank loans that are never paid. This type of scam is complex, requires an in depth knowledge of how the financial markets work and is guaranteed to be investigated by the Securities and Exchange Commission.

The Ownership Change

Companies are usually registered at the state level and some creative criminals have found that they can manipulate records on file, changing company information to their advantage, possibly adding in their own name, then applying for credit in the company's name. It's possible to find out a company's Employee Identification Number (EIN) as this is publicly available information. Once you have it, it's possible to change names on business ownership documents at the local courthouse. When you have access to their credit, you can purchase items and resell them.

Also, you could buy a business and arrange for the former owner to stay on to provide continuity to suppliers and customers. In the mean time, skim profits, run up credit and sell assets benefiting yourself. Ultimately the company will fail but your goal is for it to look to the world like it was normal business failure.

Not too long ago, a Canadian business owner received a call informing him he was late paying a utility bill for one of his office buildings. When he investigated, he found that he never received the bill because a criminal had impersonated him, changed the CEO's name to his and sold the building to an accomplice.

Similarly, some businesses are only registered in one or several states. If you find out which states a business is not registered in, you could register the business in one of these states and commit fraud.

The Vanity Scam

With the Vanity Scam, an individual sets up an organization that sounds very prestigious. They notify an executive at a corporation that they have won the top award that's offered by this bogus outfit. The unsuspecting company is told they have to pay some administrative fees in order to actually receive the award, or that they have to become a member of the prestigious organization. They are told that, once paid, the entire industry will be notified of the recognition in specific trade journals. Eager to look good and to have his company look good, the executive authorizes the payment. These payments can be ongoing in the form of administration or membership fees.

Let's say you want to target a company that produces pumps. You have identified a middle-of-the-road company, not the most reputable or the largest in the industry. Establish an organization called, say, the International Pump Association, set up a website and list on it all the pump related companies you can find, making out that they are members. Identify a new, young executive at the pump company and enquire why they have not joined, as their competitors have. Tell him that they have just completed a major survey and his employer has been voted as having the most reliable pumps on the market, sending him bogus data. The Association will be giving out an award which will be recognized nationally, but first, the pump company must join the Association and pay an administration fee to process the award. Once you have received the pump maker's fees, it's time to move on.

The Overpayment Scam

In this ruse, a purchaser overpays for an item up front with a check that eventually bounces. As soon as the check is received, they immediately ask for the overpaid amount to be refunded to them, in addition to receiving the merchandise. When the check bounces they abscond with the goods and the refunded difference. This will only work if the corporation doesn't bank your check immediately and would be best done to organizations you have a credit history with. I have read about this scam a few times but don't see this being likely to succeed. Will companies really fall for this? Apparently it has happened.

The Building Hijack

Sometimes known as address mirroring, another lucrative scheme that has been carried out is to target a corporation that occupies part of a large office building. It doesn't have to be the head office of the company, and can be one of their satellite locations. Set up a bogus company in an office in the same building. Don't put any signage on your door and keep a low profile. It may be worth bringing in some inexpensive furniture to generate the appearance of actually doing business there. Order items on credit to be sent addressed to the large corporation, but with the suite number of your business being the actual delivery address. When they arrive, resell them as new items. The large company will be billed for the items after you abscond. Items like computers and furniture are best for this type of approach, as they are relatively expensive and ordered by companies and individuals all the time. They are also relatively easy to resell. After ninety days of non-payment by the large corporation, the company you ordered from will start making noises, asking questions and demanding payment. By this time you are long gone, having loaded up your items into a moving truck and headed out of state to sell the goods. The profitability of this scheme has to be such that it greatly exceeds the rent you will be paying. However, to be most effective you won't be staying more than a few weeks. In addition to ordering items, you can establish lines of credit and order credit cards in the target company's name, then max them out.

A twist on this approach is to find a company that places orders with a specific supplier. Notify the supplier that you have set up a new facility and give them that address. Place the order for items to be shipped to the new address. The selling company will carry out the usual credit check then ship the goods to the new address: your temporary address. Let's say you want to target a distribution company that routinely orders from a janitorial supply company. You establish an address, contact the JanSan company and place an order for product, informing them that of this new shipping location. Give them a purchase order number and wait for the items to arrive.

The Fake Check

If you have access to a company's bank account number and routing number, you can print up some checks and have them written payable to yourself. Check writing software, printing equipment, ink and check stock (blank checks) can easily be purchased from multiple locations. Depositing these into your own bank account would not be smart as it's not likely to be more than a few weeks before the accounting department at the corporation notices the fraudulent withdrawal. At this point the company will either start their own investigation or notify the FBI. The Feds have amazing superpowers to locate individuals if they are motivated to do so. Simply knowing your bank account number into which you deposited the funds, they can query the bank, obtain your personal details and track you down from there. If you are going to deposit stolen funds into a bank account in your name, you need to make sure that you are completely untraceable and completely off the grid. You might be able to accomplish this by being in another country, then making sure you have access to those funds from there. Even then, the USA has agreements with most countries whereby you can be extradited and still be prosecuted. If you have a criminal record and want to return to the US from overseas, expect to be detained at the airport.

If you make the stolen amount relatively small it may not be worth the while of the company to investigate. Relatively small to one company might be relatively large to another, so you need to decide what this amount is. Embezzling large corporations, the subject of this book, I estimate that $5,000 or less might go uninvestigated. It helps to know the politics within the company ahead of time to perpetrate frauds like this. This kind of insight is best obtained by actually having worked there. You may be able to leverage an employee in the accounting department at the company you are trying to scam.

The best way to avoid capture if you plan to steal a large amount of money using fake checks is to open a bank account in someone else's name. Unfortunately, this falls squarely under the heading of identity (ID) theft and is something I do not endorse, even if it's done to your worst enemy. You could minimize any guilty feeling you may have about causing pain and suffering to others by assuming that if you transfer a large amount of money into an account set up in someone else's name, you would be using this as a pass-through account, once you deduct the funds. Walking into a bank with stolen social security number, name, address and date of birth is not the way to open accounts like this. The risk is very high that bank employees will immediately call the police who will have you arrested for bank fraud. Since doing this is very risky, one of the easier approaches to getting a bank account in someone else's name is using prepaid debit cards. There are several to choose from but one of the most popular is called Netspend. Their debit cards can be ordered from their website and sent to an anonymous address. Criminals find a suitable apartment complex where they can access the mail station and have it sent there without listing an apartment number. When mail arrives for that apartment complex, the postal employee is required to put the mail in specific boxes for each apartment. When mail arrives with no apartment number on it they will often leave it out or put it in the box of a random person. Anyone who gets mail in their box that's not addressed to them will usually set it aside in a public area. Criminals experiment by having some junk mail sent to the apartment complex of their choice to see how the process works there.

Just to be clear: this is identity theft and I am not recommending you do this. This is for illustrative purposes only.

Criminals then activate their Netspend card by going to the website and entering the stolen personal information, like SSN, date of birth, often known as Fullz. In many cases

Fullz has been stolen from databases by computer hackers and is available by paying with bitcoin on darknet markets. Netspend would run the person's profile through a database to confirm it exists. Just to restate: your goal here is not to cause any pain and suffering to the individual whose personal details you are using. You may be able to modify these techniques to open a flow-through account that you will use once, deposit a large amount into it, and then cash out. The individual whose identity is being used will be contacted by the company whose account you will be withdrawing from. They will be questioned and possibly arrested for bank fraud. In addition to the major problems caused to the victims of these identity theft crimes, you need to ask yourself how you would cash out of the fake account. Do you go to the bank where the ill-gotten funds are held and ask for cash? If so, how will you show your ID to the bank employee? If you decide to transfer the money to an account in your real name you have defeated the purpose of opening the fictitious account. Will you buy some consumer goods with funds from the fake account? If so, where will you have them shipped? Remember that all electronic transactions can be traced by the federal government, so to avoid being caught you would need to constantly stay several steps ahead of them.

The point I want to make is that attempting any kind of bank fraud using someone else's identity is like skating on very thin ice. The only way to carry this out with no consequence to anyone living is to do it using the identity of a dead person; see below section for details.

The Fake Corporation

If you're going to set up a business with the sole intent of stealing from other companies, you want to make sure that you hide behind as many layers of ownership as possible. Set up a company and make out it is a division of an existing company, but make sure you can't be traced. Set yourself up behind a maze of complex partnerships and corporations to make it as difficult as possible to be identified. Obtain business logos and get high quality business cards printed up to make yourself seem legitimate. Dress professionally and be respectful at all times as you operate. Figure out a way of appearing as nondescript as possible without any distinguishing features or a heavy accent. Establish a website for your fraudulent business with a legitimate looking email address: these days if a company is not seen to have a website or if they operate with a gmail or hotmail email address, employees in other businesses they try to transact with will not take them seriously. If you are trying to establish a fictitious company you'll want it to sound as large as possible. Good words to include in your company name include: International, US, European, Pacific, American, Global or Atlantic. A common approach is to fabricate a business that sounds similar to another more established, existing business. If there was a company legitimately doing business as Lucas Anderssen Plumbing Inc, you could generate fraudulent purchase orders and invoice as Lucas Anderssen Plumbing LLC.

If you are going to commit sophisticated scams on companies, it may be best to target businesses which are in competitive industries as they will be more likely to take risks, so less likely to be watchful of scams, making them easier targets. You might think that all industries are competitive, but when a company is selling a commodity, they compete primarily on price, rather than on selling specialized, unique or niche products. Apple would be an example of a highly profitable company that sells unique products, which are not commodities. Companies selling low price knock-off products are trying to copy a brand-name product that is established in the market place and compete by positioning their stuff as the same, only less expensive. These companies tend to have thinner profit margins, lower operating costs and consequently fewer employees who are on the look out for being scammed.

If a company is scammed, they can be very reluctant to go public with that information. It can be humiliating for the company to have this kind of bad press. They may be well known and well established in the market place and want to protect that façade. They will often notify the FBI, who will carry out an investigation but when they do this, word about the theft frequently gets out. Stock prices can tumble on such news, resulting in executives being terminated. As consumers, we are afforded a number of legal protections if our bank accounts are compromised. However, businesses have much fewer protections so are at greater risk when losses due to theft occur. You can take advantage of this.

Cyber Crime

Cyber crime techniques are not covered in this book. These include hacking into computer systems, installing malicious code onto computers, using the internet to have money wired to other companies/countries and controlling corporations electronically. Even though cyber crime is heavily publicized right now and an obvious approach to stealing from corporations, I do not endorse it. I see cyber crime as something that crosses the line into theft of personal information, resulting in suffering from individuals. The methods in this book are only designed to defraud companies and even though individuals work at these companies and may be indirectly affected by the fraudulent approaches I've documented, they are usually not affected directly. I also believe that cyber crime is one of the most prevalent crimes taking place these days and it's on the rise. The FBI and US state organizations are spending more and more resources investigating it and, I suspect, proportionately less time investigating the programs covered in this book. Cyber crime is traceable by virtue of the fact that the vast majority of electronic transactions are traceable. Avoiding that connection to your home's Internet Protocol (IP) address or media access control (MAC) address can be done using virtual private networks (VPNs), Tor and other electronic trickery, but I have serious doubts about your ability to avoid capture long term, especially from the federal government. On the other hand, if done correctly, many of the schemes presented here have less traceability due to their lack of electronic connectivity.

STEALING FROM RESTAURANTS

Restaurants are especially easy to steal small items from. Silverware, cruets and bowls easily fit in bags and in the containers they give you to take leftovers home in. Most employees there don't seem to care what you walk out with. Even though stealing from restaurants is similar to shoplifting, I find most eateries don't have any kind of loss prevention department. If you feel ambitious you can dine & dash, eating then departing before paying. On occasion I have found a problem with the restaurant, had the manager come to my table and got into a big disagreement with him, then declared: "That's it! You just bought my meal. I'm never coming here again." Then I've got up and left after I finished my food and expensive drinks. Some of these occasions were legitimate: for example, a customer at the table next to me had brought in their dog which was climbing on the seats. This was clearly not a service animal, just their pet and it was very unsanitary. After complaining to the manager, who refused to do anything about it, I stormed out. Managers will not call the police in situations like this, but will accept the loss and move on. With luck the incident will force them to give better customer satisfaction in the future.

Insurance Scams

My approach to insurance is to minimize the amount of money I give to the insurance companies. I have a minimalist lifestyle, drive inexpensive used cars, have cheap furniture in my home and buy my clothes off the clearance rack at Kohl's. Anyone looking at me or what I drive will think twice about robbing me as I don't advertise a fancy German car or expensive jewelry. And if they did try to rob me they won't find much of any value. Why do I need to spend huge amounts of money on insurance every year? I only buy the insurance that's mandatory or is going to cover a catastrophic event. I also give the insurance companies less money by carrying a high deductible.

As mentioned above, insurance claims adjusters can smell fraud from a great distance and if they're suspicious that you are trying to scam the system they won't pay you until they are satisfied. What this means is that to commit insurance fraud you need to think like them, understand how they operate and make sure your story is believable. Insurance companies are very well connected with each other. For example, if you try to get a quote for car insurance you will need to supply all kinds of personal information and they know which insurance you currently buy from other companies.

Insurance rates depend on where you live and there are some complex algorithms that insurance companies use to decide how much they are going to charge you. If you live in an expensive city it is probably worth your while registering your vehicles in a state where insurance costs are much lower. Not only can you save on insurance, but registration and taxation are much lower in some states too. There are also a number of states which do not require emissions testing of vehicles. One of the best approaches is to set up a company in Montana, using a mailing address and to have your vehicles registered there. Insurance rates are much lower there too, so if you actually live in New York City or San Francisco you can save money. If you have to make a claim while you're somewhere other than Montana, just tell the insurance adjuster that you were doing business in the more expensive place or traveling there for a vacation. State officials don't like you driving around with vehicles registered somewhere else long term. If you move to a new state they usually require you to get a local driver's license and register vehicles there within ninety days of arriving. However, if you get pulled over by the local police or have an accident, your situation can easily be explained. It becomes more challenging if you have a criminal record, so you'll want to avoid getting one of these.

Some insurance fraudsters game the system by working together to crash their vehicles, have passengers inside who claim to have serious back or neck injuries as a results and make major claims on the insurance companies. If you are going to do this, avoid doing it multiple times as insurance companies will spot trends and suspect fraud. This kind of automotive insurance fraud is well documented online if you wanted to research the details.

Getting a Debt Discount

It is astounding how much of western society is fueled by debt. Around 2008 just before the economic crash, the ratio of household debt to personal income in the USA was around 120%. That's right: there was more debt than income at that time. If you want to predict when the next major market crash will happen, this is a good indicator to watch. The average household carries around $7,000 in consumer debt. A huge percentage of society pays for all kinds of things with debt. Mortgages on homes make the most sense to have, but most other consumer debt is much less necessary than most people believe. The best approach is to have a debt-free lifestyle, but that's not always possible for everyone.

It's a little-known fact that you can get some debt forgiven. Here's how it works. If you rack up credit card bills and don't pay the entire balance off every month you will have to pay interest on your outstanding balance. Interest rates are high: typically around 16%. After a while of not paying you will be turned over to a collection agency, who will pursue you vigorously to get you to pay them. You can dodge and weave, but these people are difficult to avoid. They will demand access to your checking account. Do not give it to them. After some months of not paying you could approach them and offer to pay off, say, 25% of that debt in exchange for them canceling out the debt completely. If they agree to the verbal offer, have them write you a letter confirming the details of the debt discount deal. Do not just pay them the 25% based on a verbal agreement. This may sound like a great deal and that you're getting a lot of stuff for free, but it may not be as attractive as it sounds. Most of the 75% that you are having them discount is actually interest. But, depending on your timing, the interest rate you have and the terms you can negotiate, this could save you significantly on the purchases, as well as relieving some of your stress.

You can also do this with medical companies if you have health care debt. Let's say you had to have some expensive surgery but you didn't have health insurance. Pay off what you can slowly, then make them the same offer: you'll pay 25% of the debt, in exchange for debt forgiveness. Make sure you actually have the money you are offering, as they may not let you make this deal twice.

Most other types of debt are difficult to get forgiven. If you don't make your car payments, the financing company will repossess the car. In some cases they install a disabling device on the vehicle so they can remotely take it over or disable it if they decide you are too delinquent on your payments. In fact, it's difficult to get forgiveness on any property-related debt, like boats or houses because the creditor can just take possession of the item in question. This is not so easy with the items you bought on your credit card, or on your health care treatment. Between 2008 and 2010 when many homeowners found themselves out of work, unable to pay their mortgage debts, they found house prices had crashed and they owed more than the equity they had in the house. Some were able to get slight debt forgiveness, but mortgage companies foreclosed a lot of homes around that time.

It is very difficult to get debt forgiven by the Infernal Revenue Service (IRS). Most college loans can't be forgiven either.

Claiming Store Refunds

I don't shoplift as I have found that it's too high risk, relative to the reward that can be achieved. Most stores have a loss prevention system which includes video cameras and security guards. They have trained their staff on what to watch for. There are some simple systems you can use where you accidentally forget to check out items that were buried in your shopping cart or on the bottom of the cart that's loaded with other items. These items can be returned later for a refund. In most cases these days the universal product code (UPC), or bar code is an integral part of an item's packaging, so switching UPCs on items inside the store before paying has been made much more difficult. But if you find a big bin in a store with reduced price/clearance items, these sometimes have stickers on them. These stickers can be peeled off and placed on more expensive, but similar regularly priced items. Two piece clothing items, like bikinis, are sometimes priced for each piece. Removing one of the price tags and putting both items on the same hanger can sometimes get you two items for the price of one. You can also use some creativity if you find a store receipt. Take a look at the receipt and see what was bought. Go into the store, take some of these items off the store shelves put them into bags from the self-checkout area and exit with the receipt between your teeth. Nobody wants to touch a receipt that has been in your mouth. Alternatively, walk out of the store talking loudly and angrily into your phone.

Another scheme that has been perpetrated is when an employee works in the layaway department, a friend buys an item on layaway for a very small amount, and the employee's friend places a sticker on the item, indicating it's sold. Friend turns up and collects the item but doesn't need to pay the balance.

These are just a small selection of the more established shoplifting schemes that have been around for a long time. Experienced store managers are aware of these and many others. Be aware that you have not actually stolen anything until you leave the store without paying for it.

I prefer to recommend different types of scams relating to companies. One I came across recently involved claiming back sales tax using fake tax exemption. Not-for-profit organizations, also known as 501(c)(3) organizations, such as a schools or churches, don't pay sales tax. If they inadvertently do, they can claim it back by essentially filling out a form and submitting it to the US state government. This procedure varies by state and procedures for doing this in your state can be found online. A Texas man successfully obtained over a million dollars by claiming back Home Depot sales taxes using a fake tax exemption. He pulled this off over a period of several years. He appeared to have been claiming refunds more than once using the same receipt and may have been getting receipts from store employees.

The IRS, a part of the federal government, assigns a not-for-profit organization a National Taxonomy of Exempt Entities (NTEE) code. This number needs to be submitted to claim back sales taxes paid at the state level from the specific county in that state. Sales tax paid in one state can't be paid back through a different state. There are some items for which sales tax can't be refunded, so make sure you read the sales tax refund procedures carefully for the state you wish to claim from.

A good way to save money is to buy at bulk discount stores. Most of these require membership, but if you have a friend who is a member they can loan you their card. A friend of mine lost her membership card and had to get a new one. She then found the card she'd lost and gave it to me.

CLASS ACTION LAWSUITS

Almost every day a new class action lawsuit is filed and another one settles. These come about because companies make fraudulent claims about their products, conspire with other companies to fix prices, or break the law in other ways, all in the name of corporate greed. Now do you understand my attitude towards corporations? The good news is that companies are sometimes punished for these deeds and you can make claims against the large amounts of funds that are set aside, if you know where to look. The bad news on these class action lawsuits is that the law firms involved in handling these cases typically get one third of the settlement amounts. Another piece of bad news is that once a case has settled, there is a small window of time when you can claim. This means that unless you are constantly informed about new settled cases, you can miss out on funds that you might legally and rightfully be entitled to.

There are several companies who collect and aggregate information about these suits and publish information on their websites. Most of these do so in a way that makes the case easy to understand and, more importantly, easy to make a claim against. My favorite is Class Action Rebates, but there is also The Class Action Guide, Top Class Actions and others.

The approach you want to take here is to claim against any class action lawsuit that you can, even if you make a fraudulent claim. Class Action Rebates tells you if you need any kind of proof of purchase and how much money you might get. Where no proof of purchase is needed it's easy to claim: follow the prompts on the website, fill out the information where you'd like the money to be sent and wait patiently: it will take months for checks to arrive, often over a year. At the bottom of the form you will be required to confirm that you really did buy the product, which you may not have done. Check the box, sign your name electronically and hit the submit button. They will email you a confirmation that your claim went through. In some cases you can only make a claim by printing out a form, filling it out and mailing it to the location handling the claim, usually a law firm. However, most claims can be done online.

The suit will allege that the corporation committed the crime within a certain time frame, usually years. You will be required to state when you purchased the offending item or service. It's best to state a date right at the beginning of that period, as the company is less likely to have records going further back in time. Let's say there's a class action lawsuit where the company made and sold defective widgets between January 2001 and July 2015. Make your claim stating that you bought the defective items in January 2001.

In some cases you will be able to make a claim even if they require a proof of purchase that you don't have. Read the requirements, ask yourself what they are willing to accept and see if you can provide this. Many of them will offer you a full refund on any number of items if you can prove you bought them within a certain time period. If you don't have a receipt you can only make a lesser claim. To make the largest claim possible you may need to fabricate receipts or photographs. You may be able to find relevant photos online. One way to fabricate receipts is to scan a good quality receipt and to use good PDF-editing software to manipulate it so that it contains what is being requested. Electronic receipts of previous online purchases are easy to edit in this way. After editing and saving, print out a copy and scan it in low resolution format before uploading with the refund application form.

Some class action lawsuits are state-specific and they require you to have purchased the items when you lived in a specific state, say, California. In many cases it's still possible to make a claim, even if you don't have a California address. Submit the claim with your preferred address and make sure you say you lived in that state when the class action crime was being committed by the corporation. If they require a California address, you can find one online, possibly that of an apartment complex. Tell them that you have moved from California and now live where you want the money sent and your claim is likely to go through.

You will come across some class action lawsuits that you decide not to pursue because they are asking for information you just can't provide. Perhaps they need a specific insurance policy number that you don't have and you suspect that they will cross reference your name with that policy number in a database to decide if they will pay you. In some cases you may want to fabricate a number, but it's often not worth making these claims. Just move on to the next challenge.

Some class action sites that ask for your social security number (SSN). Even if you are making a legitimate claim you would not want to supply this, just to get a few dollars. There are a set of social security numbers which have been deemed by the federal government as non-usable. These are: 987-65-4321, -4322 etc. You can supply one of these to keep the claim moving forward. If the online system won't accept the number you have entered, submit a legitimate-looking number and work on the assumption that the law firm handling the claims may not be cross referencing names and SSNs.

Some companies are found guilty of soliciting business by faxing junk to fax machines. In order to make a claim you need to provide a fax number. You have no way of knowing if the law firm processing the claims is looking for actual fax numbers in a database, but you can provide a fax number of, say, an airline or the corporate office of a large retailer. I'd bet they received some fraudulent faxes, so you can use their number.

There will be some suits where the company was guilty of calling you when you were on a do-not-call list or when they should not have called your cell phone number. In these cases make a claim with your existing phone number or another legitimate number you have. You can even try to use someone else's phone number to see if they received these calls. Who keeps track of fake calls they receive? Sadly, I don't have the time for this, but I do receive a number of calls from companies who have got my phone number somehow. Once a company gets your phone number, they will compile a list of these and sell them to other companies as a money-making venture. I hate being pestered by getting these calls, so I feel good about making claims against companies who get busted in this way whenever I can.

Companies have found that there's money to be made by trading information and they can get this information from you in numerous unexpected ways. When I started getting phone calls from unknown numbers I called my cell phone company and asked them how I can have calls blocked. They told me they can't do it, but that there are apps that can be downloaded so that you can automatically block a number. Be very cautious about free apps that you download onto your cell phone. In exchange for downloading some apps, you allow a company to have full access to all the names, phone numbers and other contact information in your phone. Once they have this, the company can sell it to others who will solicit you. I despise this kind of shady business practice, which is one reason I encourage you to make any and every class action lawsuit claim you can.

It's also easy to make multiple class action lawsuit claims. If you can have mail sent to another address, submit a similar claim using that. If you do this, I recommend making each claim look different from every other, claiming for different amounts and spacing out the timing of the claims, so that two claims for the same person don't arrive at the lawyer's office on the same day. Don't worry about using an address that's not yours: the checks you receive will almost certainly not have an address on them. If they do, deposit them anyway. Since most claims you'll make will be made online it would be worth using a virtual private network (VPN) and changing your location's internet protocol (IP) address accordingly. If you are making a claim to come to your Chicago address, chose the Chicago IP address on your VPN. Want money coming to your Florida address? Use the Florida IP address. VPNs are extremely useful for maintaining anonymity online. There are several that are free, but since you get what you pay for in life, I have found that it's worth paying a few dollars per month for a good reliable service. Personally, I like Private Internet Access (PIA) but many others are good. PIA will allow you to purchase a one year license with a gift card, which you can buy with cash at a local store. This will give you added anonymity. Most VPN suppliers claim not to keep track of log records, IP addresses used and websites visited, but I have no way of knowing how true this is.

Class Action Rebates allows you to sign up for monthly mailings and they will email you about the latest claims you can make. In many cases the amount of money that can be claimed is small, sometimes as little as $8. You have to ask yourself how much your time is worth. It takes about ten minutes to make a typical claim. If you need to find or make receipts, the process can take longer and some claims are so simple they can be done in two minutes. If you can claim $8 for ten minutes of work, this equates to $48/hour of tax-free income.

Keep track of the claims you make and what you had to do to get them. If you see that claims you have submitted with bogus receipts are not being accepted you may need to change how you handle these. Detailed record keeping can also help you to understand other trends and subtleties regarding making claims.

Consider starting your own class action lawsuits. Every day I see products for sale and the company selling them is making claims that make me wonder how legitimate they are. If you have a product problem and feel it's likely others will have had the same problem you can gather your evidence to present to a lawyer who specializes in class action suits. If you work for a company and you know they are making fraudulent claims or making defective products, work with a friend or family member to contact a lawyer. You will get an incentive award if the suit is successful. In most cases you won't have to pay to engage the attorney as they get paid after the case is settled. They stand to make large profits if the suit settles in your favor, so this is their incentive for taking the case and not charging you up front. Class action lawsuits can be filed in situations where a group of people have been harmed physically or financially. This includes situations where your employer may have discriminated against you and some fellow employees. There are a number of websites which describe in simple terms how to start a class action lawsuit. The process starts with filling out a class action complaint and the attorney you engage has to be confident you have a strong case, so make sure you have good evidence.

As with any fraudulent activity, the risk of being caught and prosecuted for making bogus claims exists. However, if the administrators handling your submission don't like what they see the worst thing likely to happen is they will deny your claim. There is the remote possibility they will take legal action against you, but for the amount of money involved it will not be worth their while. If you are caught embezzling large amounts of money you run the risk of being prosecuted for mail fraud, a federal offense. Again, the risk of this is small as most class action lawsuit claims will be under a few hundred dollars. But the best part of all this: receiving checks in the mail, out of the blue, when you had completely forgotten you had filed the claim.

Defrauding the Health Care System

The health care system in the US is severely broken. Costs of services continue to rise by a high percentage every year for a large number of reasons. Most of the system is owned by corporations so this is another opportunity to get free services. When you need some kind of service from the medical system you almost always need to make an appointment. Before they will see you at the facility they want to understand how they'll get paid so will ask you for insurance information, which they check. I do not recommend committing identity theft and providing someone else's name and SSN as this person will be stuck with the bill, then will have to prove they don't have to pay. This causes huge inconvenience and trauma to someone. However, the health care system can be gamed at the emergency room and here is the approach. If you get injured in some way, go to the emergency room at a major hospital. Depending on how badly you are hurt they will probably admit you right away, then start diagnosing your problem. Do not take with you any identification, credit cards or any other card or document which proves who you are. At some point during the time you are there they will ask you for personally identifying information, like your name, SSN etc. Tell them you were injured at work and that you will be making a worker's compensation claim. Give them fictitious data. Make up information on the spot, while you sound delirious. Hospitals are required by law to give injured people the treatment they need, regardless of ability to pay. Before you can be released they will give you release papers and prescriptions with the bogus name you gave them. They will also give you a document requiring you to send or fax your worker's compensation information to them within a certain time period, usually three days. You will choose not to complete and return this form.

Rebates, Promotions and Recalls

Stores and manufacturers offer promotions and rebates to entice consumers into buying products that are not selling rapidly enough. The way rebates work is you buy the items, fill out a form, either on a piece of paper or online, then submit this with documentation, wait at least four weeks, then receive a check or a gift card. In most cases the rebating company has to pay a processing company anywhere from $0.40 to $1.75 to process a rebate. The rebating company realizes that it's in their interest not to have to pay out too many of them. What they want is for the consumer to buy the product or service being advertised, then to forget to send in the rebate. If they send it in, they will be careful to find a reason not to pay you. For example, if they say you have to send in the UPC from the packaging and you don't do this, or you send in the wrong UPC, they will deny your rebate claim. History has shown that retailers are more likely to avoid paying you than manufacturers. Unfortunately, it is not illegal for companies not to pay rebate claims. I know that I have submitted legitimate rebate requests over the years and just not been paid. Companies do this as they know they can get away with it.

It is possible to make fraudulent claims against companies offering rebates. As with any such claim, you need to be aware of what they need to receive in order to pay you out. There are some which actually require no proof of purchase whatsoever. These are rare, but do exist. Watch for these and be sure to apply for as many as you reasonably can with as many names and addresses as you can use. In some cases, the reward is a gift card offered by that store, which can be useful if you or your family members shop there regularly.

Another approach to watch for is where a rebate is offered but no packaging items need to be sent in. In this case you can purchase the item with cash, follow the steps needed to get the rebate money or gift card, then return the item for a full refund. If the rebate amount is significant this can be worth doing. Just like with Class Action Lawsuit claims, you need to assess the value of your time. If it takes you 15 minutes to process a $15 claim, this is equivalent to making $60 per hour.

If all that is needed to claim a rebate is to submit a receipt, you may be able to modify an existing receipt you have from that store using PDF-editing software. This can be tricky, as the company processing the rebates will be looking for specific information to appear on the receipts. Without knowing how the code numbers are established you could give them the wrong data. What you have in your favor is that the rebate processor is a third-party company who may not know all the details if you make a mistake on the receipt. Like with any schemes, there's risk that has to be weighed against reward. It will take you some time and effort to decide which approaches work and which do not. Given how long it takes to receive a rebate, it will be important for you to have good attention to detail and to practice good record keeping and documentation so you can refine your craft.

Companies make defective products regularly. Having seen manufacturing operations up close on numerous occasions I can tell you that it happens much more than you think. If manufacturers had to recall every product that was outside of specifications they would go out of business and we would all be in a sense of outrage. Manufacturers will fix up a batch of defective product as best they can and release it out into the market place if they think they can get away with it. However, if they make a product that is unsafe and they think they might get sued by consumers who could be hurt by the defect, they issue a recall. Once they have issued a recall it is more difficult to sue them for injuries, unless you can prove that you were hurt before they made the recall announcement. If you have a product that has been recalled you definitely want to go through the process they offer to make sure you get a replacement at their expense. In some cases you may be able to claim for a recall when you did not buy the product. This is usually for food items from large corporations. Follow their procedure to inform them you bought their product and had to dispose of it as you were concerned about other family members eating/drinking it and getting sick. They will usually send you several coupons for free products. Submitting fraudulent recall claims for electronics is much more difficult as they usually want you to send the defective item back to them so they can send you a replacement.

Recall information can be found online just by doing a simple internet search. The US Consumer Product Safety Commission (CSPC) website lists a large number of products being recalled. Recalls are very expensive for companies so they only do it if they really have to. In many other cases they will keep quiet about the defective product and hope they get away with it. If you hear from a friend or family member who works for a company making defective products, make sure you report it to the CSPC, which you can do through their website.

Getting Free Stuff by Complaining/Cajoling

Companies always want to keep customers happy. A happy customer is more likely to buy again. If a customer has a bad experience they will submit negative reviews in online forums or start legal action to make claims for poor products or services. Companies want to avoid this happening at all costs and this is something you can take advantage of. If you buy a product that turns out to be defective, don't just return it for an exchange. Complain. Loudly. Start by politely explaining what you are dissatisfied about and ask what the company is able to do in order to compensate you for the issue. Don't accept the first thing they offer you, as they are usually empowered to offer you more than the first offer. Make sure you tell them that you are about to submit negative online reviews, or that you are in the process of engaging your lawyer. Stress that you have been harmed physically and psychologically by the defective product and provide proof.

Claims you can make against companies will vary and sometimes the company will voluntarily offer you compensation. If you have a beer or soda can that explodes and causes some damage, make sure you take photos, keep the offending can as evidence and push for reimbursement for whatever was damaged. Some of us are somewhat leary about complaining as we don't want to create a scene or offend customer service people. A friend of mine has the perfect persistent personality for this and is a professional complainer. You can hire her out if you have an issue with an organization and she is guaranteed to get results for you.

Another friend of mine took his family to a very well-known vacation resort in Florida. While they were there they were bitten severely by bedbugs. Now, if you know anything about these creatures you know how easily they can be spread from one location to another. They like to go on trips, so if you put your bag on the bed in a hotel room they will attach themselves to the bag or climb inside, then come out at the next new location. Never put your bag on a hotel bed.

Once my friend and his family complained to resort management they were treated very well: given a debit card to buy new clothes, food and whatever they wanted, while the resort took care of heat-treating all their property to kill the bedbugs. They received a large cash payment in exchange for signing a document stating they would not go public with their story. Places like this don't like bad press.

Another way to get free stuff from companies is to hand-write them a complimentary letter, explaining how much you love their products. Given that very few people actually write letters anymore, when the customer service department receives this from you they will often be touched and write back sending coupons. There are numerous stories online of people who have done this, with Starbucks, Jimmy Johns and McDonalds allegedly being the most generous. As with other ventures like this, you have to assess the value of your time. The thrill of getting something in the mail, however, is priceless.

Car Rental Companies

Car rental companies are very profitable. They make big money, not just on the vehicle you rent from them but also on the add-ons like insurance, car seats and when they upsell you to cars with higher perceived value. The cars they have are not very well taken care of, however. The employees don't do a great job maintaining them and renters certainly don't. One of my former coworkers used to brag about how whenever he rented cars he totally thrashed them, took corners at speed, burning tires whenever he could, slammed them into a low gear driving at speed on the freeway, bumping curbs. If you ever want to buy a used car, make sure you carry out a vehicle ownership history check and never buy a car that was a rental.

Some years ago I found a used car I was interested in buying so I paid a few dollars for the history check. This car was a rental for a year, then it was sold at auction, then sold at auction, then sold at auction. The guy trying to sell it had owned it for three months. Now, I didn't know what was wrong with this car, but I knew I didn't want it based on that history.

Car rental companies can be a good way to get a good deal on some good car parts. Let's say you have a Toyota Camry and you need new tires. Go to your local car rental company and rent a Camry. Bring it home and switch the wheels. How do the spare tires compare? Make sure you have the best one. Is the stereo better in the rental? It's not too difficult to switch these out, thanks to the instant training you can get from YouTube videos. Does the rental have a newer battery or some cool accessories you covet? How do the windshield wiper blades compare? Are you missing a car jack with your Camry? Check out the trunk as the rental car will have one. Most cars I've rented don't seem to have car mats, so it's possible that renters have taken them out.

When you return the car after a day or so, the hourly-paid employee checking it in will give it a cursory inspection for body damage but won't check much beyond that, as there will be a dozen cars up behind you he needs to deal with. If the replacement parts are spotted by the car rental company some time in the future they have no way of tracing it to you, given how many other people will have rented it. If you're going to switch the wheels out I hope you don't get a car driven by my former coworker. When you rent a car, inspect it first to make sure it meets your needs based on the parts you're looking for. If it doesn't you can go back to the office and request something different.

If you are going to do this, be aware of the tiers of car rental companies. Avis and Budget are part of the same company, just different brands. Avis buys new cars and when they are about a year old they become Budget's. This is the same with Hertz, who will have newer cars, but Dollar and Thrifty get their hand-me-downs. It's similar with National/Enterprise whose cars usually go to Alamo. If you're renting to get parts you want to get a newer car.

CONFERENCES AND HOTELS

Just about every day in every major city there are numerous conferences taking place. These are usually run and funded by associations and employees from the companies who are part of the industry being represented. At these conferences you'll find a combination of talks, meetings, dinners and usually a tradeshow where exhibitors present their products to potential customers. They usually happen in convention centers or large hotels. Some cities are able to host large conventions due to their infrastructure and hotels; others are only able to host smaller events.

Crashing a convention is not difficult. Attendees can pre-register and usually pay less money for doing so, but there are usually a number of people who can't turn up for one reason or another. These people don't care about this as their employer is usually footing the bill. Conferences are rarely free, so you usually can't just fill out a form and be admitted. You want a badge from one of the no-shows and they are available to you if you know how to get them.

Do your research. Understand the nature of the conference as this will tell you how to dress. For the vast majority of these, men should wear a dress shirt, black shoes, slacks, and a sport coat. Bring a tie just in case. Ladies should wear business-appropriate attire. For videogame conventions and events attended by a younger crowd, dressing down is fine, but always make sure you are clean and presentable. Arrive at least an hour after the event has started, ideally on the second day. Most conferences take place over several days and are busiest on their first couple of days. On the final day many people leave early to go home. At smaller events the attendee badges are sitting out on a table which will be manned by a reluctant employee. Sometimes the table will be unmanned and you can take one of the badges. Other times you just have to give the name of a person whose badge you see. Rarely will the table monitor ask for any identification, but it's worth watching how badge collection goes for other people, just in case some of them require this. Bigger conferences don't have enough table space to have badges laid out on display so you have to go to the pre-registration desk and ask for them.

Once inside the conference you can often eat at no charge for the duration of the event. Conferences usually have some kind of large networking event with free food and drinks.

It can be fun to go there with a friend, meet people and pretend to be someone else. Many vendors have giveaways, but these are usually cheap trinkets which might be good to give to children. If you need free pens, squishy toys and USB memory sticks, this is the place to get dozens.

Make sure you take business cards with you to drop into fishbowls for drawings. I have won some cool swag from these. I've seen how companies decide who has won these raffles and it's not as equitable as you might think. The reason companies offer to raffle off a cool item like an iPad or a drone is not to be altruistic. They are doing it to attract attention to the booth in the hope of getting more customers. At the end of the event, some of the people running the booth will get together to decide who has "won" the drawing. They do this by sifting through the business cards and discarding any that would not be a customer. Then they decide who has won, often by putting the cards back in the fishbowl and randomly drawing from the narrower field. Sometimes they just decide they like a particular person, or that he would be a promising new prospect they'd like to influence and they give the prize to him. So if you want to win swag from a raffle at a trade show, make sure your business card is printed to make out you're a customer. It's easy to print up credible business cards on your computer.

It's unusual for products to be sold at conferences, but be aware of the mentality of the people at the trade show booths: they are looking to connect with new customers. If you are persuasive enough, you can game yourself into their organization and use other tricks I've documented in this book.

The vast majority of people at a conference or convention are from somewhere else, so need to stay in hotels. Hotels get very busy during these times. Hotel managers and employees are used to seeing professionally-dressed people in their hotels, many of whom won't be staying there, so they won't be paying attention to you if you look like all the rest. This is your opportunity to scope out the hotels for anything that might be lying around. If you're staying in a hotel room, be aware that the vast majority of hotels do not track towels, sheets, coat hangers or any of the toiletries you'll find in the bathroom. This means that you can take these with minimal risk. Housekeeping staff are overworked and when they come into a room to clean it, if they see a pile of sheets or towels on the floor they will pick up the entire pile and drop it into their laundry cart. If it happens to be missing a few things they rarely notice or care. Televisions are always bolted down and much too large to squeeze into a suitcase. Just like furniture, it will be obvious if it's missing. Some small safes are bolted down to a sturdy piece of furniture with bolts that can sometimes be removed from inside or underneath the safe. Moving one of these out of the hotel on a luggage cart along with the rest of your stuff might be feasible. Small microwave ovens are about the same size, so could also be taken.

Many hotels offer breakfasts as part of the hotel stay. These are not free, but are included in the price that the guests pay. It is usually possible to walk into a one of these hotels around breakfast time and eat at no charge. Make sure that you dress appropriately and look like you're actually staying there. Don't wear a hat, coat or gloves as you walk into the breakfast area as this will send a message that you aren't a guest there. As with many other scams, make sure you look confident, as if you belong there. Visualize yourself having just spent the night in one of their comfortable beds.

SOCIAL ENGINEERING

Social engineering is the art of persuading others to do something they would not normally do. It's a relatively new term that encompasses a wide variety of confidence tricks, where the objective is to gather information, gain access to systems or facilities, or just get money or goods. At some time or another you will need to develop good social engineering skills if you are planning to scam corporations. It helps if you have good people skills, are naturally persuasive and have the ability to lie and be convincing, as this is at the heart of good social engineering. We all do this to some extent. Think about the times when you were young and needed your parents to take you somewhere. Or when you tried to get your first job and had to convince the hiring manager you could handle it. Or when you wanted to go on a date with someone. Every day we face situations where we need to be able to convince someone to do something.

Start by visualizing yourself getting whatever it is you want. Imagine how you are going to achieve this and who you need to convince. Realize that whomever you need to persuade has wants, needs and desires too and they will not take kindly to being verbally abused, but are more likely to help you get what you want if you are viewed as a considerate person who has a need. Remember that people do business with and are willing to work with other people who they know, like and trust. The person you are working with needs to know you and a few things about you. It often helps to establish a common bond between you and the person you are trying to socially engineer. This could be the state you both lived in, where you have both vacationed, people you both know or some other common interest you can ferret out. If you have the opportunity to do some research on the person you need to get help from, this will speed up the social engineering process.

When trying to convince others to do something, it's important to be calm, polite but persistent. Sometimes you'll get objections, so just politely restate your request or position. Once you've firmly but politely made your statement three times in a row the other person will often see your determination and either give you what you want, or won't.

If you try to conduct social engineering by phone, one challenge can be just getting the person you are calling to answer and speak to you. One useful utility here is FIRErtc, which allows you to spoof your actual caller ID. Download the free app, decide which company you want to pretend to belong to and use your PC or smart phone to make calls. There are other phone apps like this available.

Entire books have been written on the subject of social engineering and the purpose of this section is not to reproduce other works, but to make you aware that it's something you need to be good at if you are to successfully scam corporations. Only people who want to live dull lives on the straight and narrow don't need these skills. I believe there's a very thin line between what is right and wrong, legal and illegal, ethical and immoral. It's much more exciting to live life close to that line.

DIE!

Something else to consider is how you may be able to let your beneficiaries truly benefit from your life by not having them notify the authorities of your death. Suppose you become terminally ill and know you only have a short time to live. Make arrangements for your beneficiaries to have your money in joint accounts. Sell any property they won't need and transfer other property, such as real estate, into joint accounts with them. Choose which other country you'd like to spend your dying days in, say, Argentina. Make yourself comfortable there with some loved ones to take care of you. When you pass away, have your beneficiaries perform a brief ceremony and dispose of your body discretely. If your body is found, there will be no dental or other records relating to you in that country for them to identify your body, so your death would be classified as Unidentified Decedent (UID). Have your beneficiaries not report your death in the USA and give them a gift they will always remember: your identity. They will have full access to your joint accounts and can transfer funds from these into their own accounts as they need to. Let them make withdrawals from your Individual Retirement Accounts (IRAs) and 401(k) funds, which you personally couldn't transfer to anyone without liquidating them and incurring tax penalties. These funds can also be deposited into the joint accounts. Allow them to open up credit cards in your name, max them out and default. Give them permission to steal funds from corporate bank accounts and use your bank accounts for pass-through purposes. Have them deposit your social security checks into one of the joint accounts for them to share. Social security needs to occasionally revalidate your situation to make sure they are paying out correctly. If your beneficiaries want to continue to receive funds they may have to commit fraud on some forms. It will be difficult for the authorities to apprehend you from beyond the grave.

It will be very important to have just the right kind of relationship with your beneficiaries for this approach to work ideally. You need to be able to totally trust them while you are still alive so that they don't liquidate your joint accounts. They need to be able to work together during and after your death so that one doesn't take advantage of another. They also need to be open to committing the type of crimes that I'm describing here. Not everyone is comfortable doing this and it may eat away at them and make them uneasy. You would need to make sure you fully understand your beneficiaries while you are alive to be sure you can trust them after your death.

A challenge you'll have is satisfying the curiosity of friends and other relatives who wonder where you are, not being aware that you're dead. Your beneficiaries could explain that you've decided to settle in Argentina. There are a few variations you could make to this approach. Your beneficiaries might decide that fraudulently claiming social security is too risky and they only want to take your retirement savings and max out your credit cards. In many, if not all states it is illegal not to declare a death, so your beneficiaries need to be well aware of what they are getting into. Depositing someone else's social security checks into a joint account will work for a while, but your beneficiaries need to ask themselves what happens when they decide to stop? There will be an electronic paper trail with the deposits into the joint account, then into your beneficiary's accounts, which The Feds can investigate if they are motivated to do.

HAVING A LIFELONG GOAL

The kind of creative lifting described in this book can be exhilarating and rewarding. If carried out over a long time period it can subsidize your lifestyle and add a significant percentage to your take-home pay. I recommend setting up and running your operation as if it were a business. Keep records so you can refer back to how things were when you started and you can see how you have progressed. Make sure that any documentation is written in a way that only you can understand, in case it falls into the hands of someone else. One of the Nazis' downfalls was that they documented everything. When World War 2 ended and the Allied Forces started their investigations into what happened there was a clear paper trail.

I like to use code names for projects. Let's say I wanted to document my class action lawsuit claims. I might call that project Arthur. Maybe I had a cousin by that name who was a victim in a lawsuit some years ago and that stuck in my mind. Let's say I took money from employers: I might label those papers Tami. Maybe Tami was a coworker I slept with a few times while I was there. If some nosy person came across a paper that had the name Arthur at the top and had some scribbled dates and dollar amounts on it and it was stuffed inside a 2009 medical benefits folder, they might ignore it.

Summary

Some years back when I was young and naïve I had this vision that the world was a perfect place. Everything was orderly, people were always decent and crime was perpetrated by bad people who made up a tiny percentage of the population. I have since found that life is not that way. It's easy to categorize people into one of two groups: good or bad; black or white; Republican or Democrat; straight or gay. People are not either good or bad. We're all in this world together and adapt to our environments. At varying times in our lives we become opportunistic in different ways for different reasons. Whether you pursue any of the techniques in this book depends on where you are in life and how bold and opportunistic you want to be.

When you work for a corporation, feel free to practice topics outlined in Part One. Even when you are employed, you can still practice those things covered in Part Two on other companies. Remember the importance of treating people as you'd like to be treated yourself, not stealing from individuals, not-for-profits or small businesses. Capitalize on the corporations who are out to capitalize on you. And remember to give as much assistance to those around you who are also trying to achieve these goals and in many cases struggling just to get by.

If you have any feedback or want to discuss any points privately please reach me through my website:

www.HowToScamCorporations.weebly.com.

Best Regards,
Lucas Anderssen

Also by Lucas Anderssen: **Corporations Suck: Beat Them At Their Own Game**

Notes

www.ingramcontent.com/pod-product-compliance
Lightning Source LLC
Chambersburg PA
CBHW020436220526
45464CB00002B/727